Naturally Delicious Desserts

Naturally Delicious
DESSERTS

Cherie Baker

BALLANTINE BOOKS   NEW YORK

Contents

ACKNOWLEDGMENTS

Writing a cookbook turned out to be a more awesome task than I ever expected, and many people helped me along the way. Thanks to family and friends whose support and guidance were instrumental in the writing (and completing!) of this book. And, for their patience and kindness, thanks to my editors, Marilyn Abraham (who made the book a reality), Pat Connell, and Ginny Faber. Special thanks go to Jeanne Drewsen and Molly Russakoff, and, to the Yarrowstalk restaurant, where the inspiration for many of these recipes was born.

Naturally Delicious Desserts

Introduction

I love dark, rich devil's food cake, gloriously frosted with buttercream rosettes. I adore chocolate chip cookies, cinnamon buns aswim in melted butter, and cream cheese hearts smothered in hot raspberry sauce. So why do I shake convulsively at the mere thought of these luscious delights? Our tastebuds were introduced to sweets by means of sugared commercial baby food and bottles filled with fruit juice. A brightly colored lollipop was a great pacifier—even at the dentist's. As children, most of us salivated at the first sight of these treats, which were often used as rewards for good behavior and are still fond reminders of birthdays and holidays. A popular board game, Candyland, and a favorite bedtime story, "Hansel and Gretel" reinforced our sweet dreams. In adolescence our sugar fantasies were satiated with more candy bars, ice cream, and soda. The perils of overindulgence were only considered as they affected our vanity—through weight gain or cavities. At the same time we were passionately fond of such foods as potato chips and French fries. Unfortunately, we did not comprehend how our carefree consumption of these foods could eventually affect not only our physical appearance but, more importantly, our health for the rest of our lives.

As adults, most of us are aware of the relationship between diet and good health. We know that sugar is nasty when our favorite pants don't zip or when the dentist intones, "Root canal!" We also have a general idea that fats are responsible for pudginess and "the greasies." However, for some of us there are much more serious, long-term effects from imprudent eating. Medical studies have linked diets high in saturated fats and cholesterol and highly processed foods with cardiovascular disease. And all fats, not simply saturated fats, have been linked to certain cancers. Though the claim is still highly controversial, some doctors think that sugar may play a role in mental disorders. And of course, it has long been known that sugar provides only calories, no nutrients.

We have been advised to reduce our intake of these culprit foods. In the United States, where it is not uncommon for an adult to consume 120 pounds of refined sugar per year, where foods rich in saturated fats and cholesterol (eggs, cheese, butter, and red meats) are the staples of our everyday diet, and where fast food chains are often the only choice on the highway, this advice may be well intended but difficult to put into practice. Some doctors and nutritionists suggest that the sugars in our diet should be predominantly from natural sources. But for many people desserts do more than simply satisfy our taste buds; they also play a central role in social traditions. Must we become accustomed to the idea of birthday candles emerging from a bowl of fruit? Is it inevitable that to be healthy one must face a lifetime of dessert denial?

This book was written with such questions in mind. It offers delicious and nutritious alternatives, with a touch of French pastry elegance, to the traditional American dessert menu. The recipes in this book do not include refined sugars or flours or any ingredients containing chemical additives. They also do not include any foods of animal origin; they are, therefore, suitable for the totally vegetarian diet.

Unlike desserts containing highly refined ingredients, these recipes contribute more than just calories: They also supply valuable nutrients. However, keep in mind that they are not a panacea for the gluttonous sweet tooth. Although some of these desserts are lower in calories than their standard counterparts, when consumed to excess the calories still add up and can lead to weight gain. And because many of the grain sweeteners used in the recipes are rich in simple sugars, these recipes should not be used by diabetics or hypoglycemics, except with the approval of a physician.

The ingredients used here may be new and different to some readers, but don't let unfamiliar names dissuade you from exploring exciting desserts and diet possibilities. These ingredients should not be thought of as imitations of such unique tastes and textures as chocolate, butter, or cream; they should be enjoyed for their own flavorful qualities.

It is comforting to know that for those of us still caught in Candyland, and not quite ready for just an-apple-a-day, there are sinfully delicious and nutritious alternatives.

You can have your cake and eat it too!

Ingredients

W hen a dessert book does not include such classic ingredients as eggs, cream, butter, and granulated sugar, there had better be some good reasons. Some ingredients, such as refined sugars, have been excluded from these recipes because they are lacking in nutritive value. Dairy products, though a good source of protein and nutrients, have also been excluded because many of these foods are high in saturated fats, suspected culprits in hardening of the arteries. Various other foods of animal origin have not been used, in deference to the increasing number of people who, for moral, religious, or economic reasons, choose not to include them in their diet. Though no 100 percent guarantee of purity is even possible, the recommended ingredients used in these recipes are from natural sources and can be generally assumed not to contain man-made chemicals, preservatives, colors, or flavors. They provide greater nutritional value than their conventional counterparts.

COOKING FATS:
Butter and Lard, Margarine, and Vegetable Oils

In desserts and baked goods, fats have traditionally been used as shortenings to give a flaky quality to piecrusts and a rich, buttery flavor to cakes and cookies. Saturated fats, such as butter, lard, and suet, are solid at room temperature; the more saturated a fat is, the more solid it will be. These fats are prized by cooks for the special qualities they impart to baked goods. Unfortunately, they have been linked in some medical studies to elevated cholesterol levels in the blood, which in turn are implicated in hardening of the arteries. Although saturated fats are found primarily in foods of animal origin, they are also abundant in coconut oil and palm oil, which are used extensively in commercial baked goods. While most doctors agree that a number of factors contribute to heart disease, there is clear evidence that animal foods high in saturated fats and cholesterol play a determining role. Therefore, it is wise to decrease one's intake of fatty foods and to avoid shortenings such as butter and lard. Desserts are a logical and surprisingly easy place to start.

Margarine has become a popular replacement for butter and other saturated fats. Margarine and butter have approximately the same nutritional and caloric value. Look for partially hydrogenated margarine made from corn, safflower, or soybean oil. Various vegetable oils have also been gaining in popularity in recent years. Vegetable oils contain no cholesterol, and most are high in unsaturated fat. They provide an alternative shortening in a totally vegetarian diet. These oils are extracted from nuts, seeds, and vegetables; the most common oils available to the consumer are safflower, corn, peanut, soybean, sesame, olive, and coconut. Oils highest in polyunsaturates are safflower, corn, soybean, and sunflower. Coconut oil is extremely saturated (but makes a great hair conditioner!).

Polyunsaturated vegetable oils supply linoleic and linolenic fatty acids, two important substances that must be provided by dietary intake since they cannot be synthesized by the body. These fatty acids help to maintain body membranes and maintain cholesterol metabolism. Since polyunsaturated oils are particularly susceptible to rancidity, they should be refrigerated after opening.

EGGS AND EGG SUBSTITUTES

Eggs are often referred to as nature's most perfect food, supplying an important source of high-quality protein. But egg yolks play a large role in the cholesterol controversy. One average yolk contains 252 milligrams of cholesterol, yet the recommended daily limit for an adult is only 300 milligrams. When one considers the number of eggs consumed in three typical daily meals, one can see that this limit is easily surpassed. For those who have been advised to restrict their dietary intake of cholesterol or who wish to practice a bit of preventive medicine, the use of eggs in desserts or baked goods should be avoided whenever possible.

The idea of eggless desserts may initially seem impossible, since eggs serve three important functions in baking: The egg yolk acts as a binder that thickens when heated; the egg white adds volume and lightness as a leavening agent; and the whole egg adds rich, moist texture. But there are alternatives that are not only cholesterol-free, but flavorful and nutritious as well.

Alternative binders can be made from nuts, various flours, starches, and cooked beans. As binders they serve the same purpose as egg yolks—that is, they act as emulsifiers that bind with fat-free liquids and keep them from separating. Nut butters are made from nuts or seeds that are ground with oil to a paste consistency. They are a highly concentrated food, rich in protein and polyunsaturated fats (except for peanut butter, which is predominantly mono-unsaturated), but also high in calories. Their nutritional content varies depending on the nuts used, but nut butters are generally good sources of fiber, B vitamins, iron, vitamin E, and trace minerals. Since these butters are very rich, they should be used sparingly; in most dessert recipes only a few tablespoons are necessary as a binder. Many nut and seed butters, such as almond, cashew, peanut, and sesame, can be purchased in health food stores. However, it is more economical to make them at home with the help of a blender or food processor. Nut butters can be used not only as binders but also as fillings for tarts and cakes. When piped through a decorative pastry tube they replace a sugary frosting.

Binders can also be made from various flours mixed with water and blended into a paste; they can either be used immediately or cooked and then stored in the refrigerator. Quick binders can be made from garbanzo, soy, oat, or brown rice flour; a few tablespoons added to cake, cookie, or dessert bread recipes contributes a delicious flavor. Soy binders should be cooked to improve their taste and digestibility.

Arrowroot is a starch derived from the roots of a South American tropical plant. It makes an excellent thickener or binder. When mixed with water, arrowroot is used to replace cornstarch, which is a highly refined thickener traditionally favored for pie fillings, fruit glazes, and translucent sauces. When substituting arrowroot for cornstarch, use the same amount—approximately one tablespoon of arrowroot will thicken one cup of liquid.

Kuzu is a high-quality starch imported from Japan, where it has been used for centuries as a remedy for stomachache, fatigue, and intestinal problems and as an aid to general good health. Because it is a relatively pure product and easily digested (unlike cornstarch), its use as a thickener has increased. Kuzu powder may be highly processed with chemical bleaches and drying agents, but the kind sold in health food stores is usually in its pure form. When substituting kuzu powder for either arrowroot or cornstarch, reduce the starch by a third. One teaspoon of kuzu powder will thicken one cup of liquid. (If an acid liquid, such as apple cider or citrus juice, is used, then slightly increase the amount of kuzu.)

Lecithin, a fatlike substance most often derived from the soybean, is sold in health food stores in both liquid and granular form. It is an effective binder because it acts as an emulsifier, keeping usually immiscible fats and liquids from separating when mixed. Liquid lecithin is preferable because it is less highly refined than the granular form. It can also be used to "grease" cookie or cake pans. The nonstick sprays marketed as fat-free alternatives for greasing cookware are actually made with lecithin.

Flaxseed gel is a mucilaginous substance that is derived from soaking, simmering, and straining flaxseeds. These seeds have been used in Europe for centuries as nutritious additions to delicious breads. The thick liquid that is strained from the seeds is refrigerated and then whipped like egg whites, after which it can be folded into mousses and frostings as a binder or used as a meringue topping. However, flaxseed gel cannot withstand the heat of baking or cooking.

Yet another thickener, agar-agar, is a gelatinous substance derived from seaweed. Often packaged under the product name of kanten, it is a vegetable substitute for gelatin (which is made from powdered cow or horse hooves). Unlike gelatin, agar-agar's thickening strength is not weakened by acids or exposure to heat. It is sold in bar, flake, or powder form; I prefer the flakes because they are easier to measure and slightly less expensive. There are only a few brands of agar-agar or kanten that have not been highly purified with chemicals and processing. These are available in most health food stores.

Carrageenan, or Irish moss, is also derived from seaweed. Its use originated in Ireland, but it is now obtained from seaweed found off the coast of Maine. Carrageenan has a considerable mineral content and is added to some "health foods" for its preservative qualities. However, its thickening ability will weaken when used with acidic fruits. It can usually be purchased in powdered form from natural food or herb and spice stores.

LEAVENING AGENTS:
Baker's Yeast and Fermented Starters

When eggs are not used, there are alternative leavening agents for light, fluffy cakes and breads. Baker's yeast is available in compressed cakes or "active dry" granules, which can be used interchangeably. Although it is commonly used as a leavener in breads and pastries, it can also be used in cakes to replace baking soda or powder. Yeast is a living organism that feeds on either the natural sugars in the flour or on an added sweetener. Upon metabolizing sugar the yeast produces carbon dioxide gas, which causes the dough to rise and expand. Baker's yeast is especially valuable when used with whole wheat flour or white flour with extra bran added. Bran contains phytic acids, substances that attract important minerals such as calcium, iron, and zinc and carry them through the digestive tract before they can be properly absorbed. Baker's yeast contains phytase, an enzyme that breaks down phytic acids and thus allows the minerals to be digested and utilized by the body.

Fermented "starters" were used for leavening long before yeast could be purchased commercially. These starters can be made with potato-cooking water, cornmeal and water, or other broth-type mixtures, which provide a nutrient medium for wild airborne yeasts.

SWEETENERS:
Granulated Sugars, Molasses, Honey, Maple Syrup, Fructose, and Natural Grain Sweeteners

Granulated sugars are commonly used ingredients in many of our favorite cakes, cookies, ice creams, and other sweets. White, brown, and powdered sugars are now considered staples in our everyday diet but were once available only for special occasions, and only to those who could afford them. After the turn of the century, technology lowered the cost of producing refined sugar and as a result dramatically increased its availability and use. Sugar is added by many food manufacturers to canned, frozen, or otherwise prepackaged convenience foods. As a consequence, frequent users of such products can consume over 120 pounds of sugar a year—approximately one pound of sugar every three days. Sugar is often consumed at the expense of other more nutritious foods, and excess sugar in the diet has been linked with such health problems as obesity, tooth decay, and, most recently, raised triglyceride levels that may contribute to heart disease in carbohydrate-sensitive individuals. Because refined sugar contains no dietary fiber, it is absorbed more quickly than the sugar in fruits. This can cause sharp swings in the blood sugar level. Headaches, irritability, and fatigue can result, although, admittedly, only some people experience this problem.

White table sugar—sucrose, the ever popular sweetener used in practically all households—is one of the least nutritious foods available. The sucrose obtained from sugar cane (or sugar beets) is the most refined result of the process that ultimately yields a variety of our commonly used sweeteners. After sugar cane is pressed, its juices are chemically purified and then cooked until crystallization occurs. The remaining juices are removed from the crystals in a series of extractions. The first extraction results in "raw" or Demerara turbinado sugar. (True raw sugar is no longer sold, since it may be contaminated with insect parts and chemical residues.) Although turbinado sugar was once advertised as nutritionally superior to white sugar, it is actually 99 percent sucrose.

The second and third cane extractions produce molasses, which is formed of the residue remaining after most of the sucrose has been removed from the sugar cane. Molasses contains significant amounts of calcium, iron, and chromium, but may also contain traces of pesticides and sulfur. Blackstrap molasses is the final product in sugar refinement and therefore contains the least sucrose; it is nutritious, but can also contain the greatest concentration of contaminants.

Brown sugars are produced by adding various amounts of molasses to granulated sugar. While the molasses adds a small quantity of trace minerals, these sweeteners are still mostly sucrose.

Honey has long been the sweetheart of sugar substitutes. It is a natural sweetener taken directly from beehives and it undergoes very little processing. The honey sold in supermarkets has usually been heated and filtered to remove any pieces of the waxy comb or pollen. (This process also keeps the honey from fermenting and thus increases its shelf life.) Honey is also available in its raw, unheated, or "organic," form and sold on the comb, which purportedly protects its nutritive value. But despite its proponents' claims, honey has an insignificant mineral content and is, in fact, nutritionally extremely similar to white sugar; both honey and sucrose are made up of glucose and fructose, although in different proportions. Honey is at least as likely as sucrose to contribute to cavities because it is a syrup and tends to stick to the teeth.

Maple syrup, another natural sweetener, is maple tree sap that has been boiled down to syrup consistency. Most maple syrup in this country is produced in Vermont; Canadian syrup is also available. Although it is a natural sugar that undergoes little processing other than boiling, pure maple syrup contains 66 percent sucrose and should therefore be avoided by diabetics. However, unlike white sugar, it may also contain significant amounts of calcium and trace minerals. Look for pure maple syrup without preservatives.

Fresh fruits are considered the healthiest means of satisfying a craving for sweets. Most fruits provide at least one or more important nutrients. Fruits contain a combination of sugars, including fructose, glucose, and sucrose. Scientists believe that the sugar in fruits has a less pronounced effect on the blood sugar level. Why? First, because fructose, one of the sugars in fruit, seems to be absorbed more slowly than these other sugars. Another reason is that fruits contain certain forms of dietary fiber that slow the absorption of sugars, keeping the blood sugar at a more constant level.

While they vary in nutritional content, fruits are generally good sources of natural sugars, vitamin C, and fiber. Unfortunately, there are other factors that shadow the benefits of fresh fruits. Although the skin of the fruit is where many of the nutrients are concentrated, it may also retain pesticide residues. There are "organically grown" fruits sold in many natural foods stores, but these fruits are more expensive, and there is no guarantee that they are chemical-free. All fruit should be washed thoroughly before you eat it.

Fruit juices are used in many of the recipes in this book—the more freshly pressed the better, because even under refrigeration their nutrient content diminishes within forty-eight hours. Unsweetened "fresh-frozen" fruit juices may be just as nutritious as home-pressed, since they are usually squeezed and frozen soon after harvest.

Dried fruits are a favorite addition to many desserts, but their natural sugars are highly concentrated and in some people can upset blood sugar levels when consumed in large quantities. When added to desserts dried fruits reduce the need for other sugars.

Date sugar is sold in some health food stores. It is a highly concentrated sugar made from dehydrated dates that are finely ground to a granular consistency. Date sugar is minimally processed and is, therefore, considered one of the most "natural" sweeteners. It contains significant amounts of calcium, iron, and vitamin A, plus some trace minerals. It is occasionally used for decoration in the recipes in this book.

Sorghum syrup (or sorghum molasses) is made from sweet sorghum, a tall grass of the millet family. It undergoes little processing: The stalks are crushed, and the resulting sweet juice is boiled down into a syrup containing natural sucrose. Sorghum molasses is available in some health food stores. While more expensive than other natural grain sweeteners, it provides a lighter-tasting alternative, especially during the transition from granulated sugars.

Natural sweeteners are made from various grains and are sold in most health food stores. They are lightly processed from barley, rice, wheat, and corn. The grain is sprouted, or malted, and allowed to ferment from starch to natural sugar. The result is a sweet liquid that is cooked down into a syrup. These sweeteners are significantly more nutritious than table sugar, but are also highly concentrated sugars and should not be used by diabetics or hypoglycemics unless approved by their physician or dietician. Barley malt is the least sweet and the least expensive of the grain sweeteners. In baking, a mixture of barley malt and pure corn syrup (that is, syrup produced from sprouted corn, not from highly refined cornstarch) is preferable to 100 percent barley malt because the mixture is sweeter and more mildly malt flavored. This can be purchased in health food stores. Rice syrup is the lightest grain sweetener in flavor and color; it is also the most expensive. Amasake is a grain syrup that can easily be made at home (page 166), making it the most economical of all. Although it can be made from any grain, amasake made from sweet brown rice is the best type for desserts. The rice is mixed with koji, a rice grain that has been inoculated with a mold that helps turn starch into sugar; the longer the mixture is allowed to ferment, the sweeter the syrup will be. The syrup can be used as a sweetener or thickened into a pudding.

The choice of sweetener will ultimately depend on one's own taste, developed through experimenting with various dessert recipes. Keep in mind that excessive consumption of sugar, whether natural or refined, can be detrimental to health. However, I can say from experience that after a period of using only grain sweeteners, my craving for sweets has been greatly reduced.

FLAVORINGS:
Chocolate, Carob, Coffee, Flavor Extracts, and Spices

Chocolate may well be the most revered of all flavors commonly used in desserts. It is made from roasted cacao seeds, which are ground and sold as a variety of products including cocoa butter, powdered cocoa, and chocolate squares and bars of varying sweetness. While chocolate is treasured by many as a delicious confection, it is often consumed with more than a little guilt. Chocolate has been associated with acne and weight gain due to its high fat content (40 to 60 percent). However, chocolate can be considered a nutritious food because fats supply more than twice the calories per gram than proteins or carbohydrates (although most of us do not need the extra calories!). Chocolate and cocoa are also good sources of iron, potassium, and trace minerals. In recent dental studies, chocolate has been shown to have a "decay-inhibiting property." While these favorable aspects of chocolate may delight the rationalizing "chocoholic," there is also a bittersweet side to the story. Chocolate contains undesirable components, such as caffeine, tannins, and oxalic acid. Caffeine is found naturally not only in chocolate and cocoa, but in coffee and tea, although the amount in chocolate is substantially lower. Tannins are a natural coloring agent found in chocolate, cocoa, tea, coffee, and carob. They are suspected of inhibiting growth of laboratory animals. Chocolate and cocoa also contain oxalic acid, which disrupts the body's absorption of calcium.

Carob powder or flour is made from the pod of the carob tree. Its flavor is a bit similar to chocolate, especially when lightly roasted. Carob has become a popular substitute for chocolate not only for its flavor, but also because it is low in fat and does not contain caffeine. It also contains small amounts of protein and calcium. It is naturally sweet, which lessens the need for additional sugars in desserts.

Coffee adds a delicious mocha taste to many desserts, and like chocolate, its unique flavor is difficult to replace. Coffee contains caffeine, tannins, and some essential oils that may stimulate gastric juices, which in some people can cause upset stomach. People suffering from peptic ulcers, gastritis, and hiatus hernia are often advised to avoid coffee. Decaffeinated coffee offers one alternative to the caffeine problem but still contains the irritating oils. Decaffeinated coffees may also contain residues of solvents used in their processing, the safety of which is still being tested. Some speciality food stores sell a decaffeinated coffee processed by means of a "water" method, which does not leave chemical residues. If one wishes to avoid coffee entirely, there are substitutes available that are blended from such sources as malted barley and chicory.

A number of flavor extracts both natural and synthetic are available to the public. Among the natural flavor extracts commonly used in desserts are vanilla, almond, anise, orange, lemon, mocha, and peppermint. Pure extracts are made by steeping various substances in alcohol. While the word *pure* implies "healthy," when it comes to flavor extracts this may not always be the case. Safrole, a root beer flavor naturally derived from the sassafras root, was removed from the market when it was found to cause liver cancer and extensive organ damage in laboratory animals. Calamus oil, another naturally derived flavoring from the calamus root (sometimes used in candy), was also banned after it was shown to cause cancer.

Spices play an important role in the flavoring of many desserts. Some of the most popular dessert spices are cinnamon, nutmeg, ginger, cloves, and allspice. Other more exotic spices include Chinese cinnamon, star anise, and cardamom. Spices may lose their flavoring strength after prolonged exposure to heat and light and should be stored in opaque airtight containers. In many cases they may be purchased in whole form and freshly grated or ground for each use.

Salt is used in dessert recipes for a variety of reasons: to complement other flavorings, as a preservative, and to help set puddings or mousses. However, salt has been cited as an overused food additive that is responsible for a variety of health problems. Salt contributes to high blood pressure, which can lead to heart attack, stroke, and congestive heart failure. Excessive salt consumption also contributes to water retention. The body's daily sodium requirement is small and usually far exceeded by sodium in the diet. Salt is excluded from most of the recipes in this book. Margarine, used as a shortening in some of these recipes, contains sufficient sodium to preclude the use of additional salt. For those on salt-free diets, unsalted margarines made from polyunsaturated oils are now available in supermarkets.

A few recipes have been included that use unsweetened chocolate, cocoa, and carob for those special occasions when only these flavors will do. The only flavor extracts used in this book are almond and vanilla; when available, a vanilla bean is better still. Vanilla beans can be purchased in shops that sell coffee, tea, and spices and in some natural foods stores. A one-inch piece, split open to release the seeds, is equivalent to one teaspoon of pure vanilla extract. Honey and maple syrup are also used as flavorings. Amasake, used as a sweetener, can add a pleasant liqueurlike taste to dessert sauces and holiday fruitcakes. Freshly ground spices really make a difference in flavor, especially in recipes using less sweetener and little or no salt. Dry white wine that contains only natural sugars from fermented grapes can be used to poach pears and other fresh fruits (unless one has special dietary restrictions). Fresh fruit juices and the juices extracted from dried fruits rehydrated in water can also be used for flavoring.

FLOURS:
Bleached or Unbleached White Flour, Whole Wheat Flour, and Other Whole Grain Flours

Whole wheat and whole grain flour products are generally considered to be superior to refined white flour in nutrients and flavor. Although white flour is "enriched" with some of the nutrients that were lost in the refining process, it loses much of its bran and fiber content. The bran that is removed is sold as a separate product. Wheat germ, the most nutritious part of the wheat kernel, is removed because it contains oils that can become rancid.

The recipes in this book use various combinations of whole wheat and other flours. If you are unaccustomed to the grainier textures of these flours (and have always used all-purpose white flour) then experiment with these recipes, starting with the lighter flours—unbleached all-purpose white and whole wheat pastry. This is also advisable for those people whose diets do not include other whole wheat or grain products, as an abrupt switch to a fiber-filled diet may cause digestive upset. However, eventually the body will adjust, and the palate will be "spoiled" forever by the delicious, full-flavored tastes and textures of whole-grain flours. As the popularity of these flours continues to grow, more natural food stores and even supermarkets are beginning to carry a wider variety. However, whole-grain flours contain natural oils that can quickly turn rancid under poor storage conditions. Flours with a high fat content, such as full-fat soy, peanut, and wheat germ, must be refrigerated and should be dated for freshness; do not buy any such flour that is over two weeks old. If you do not have access to stores selling whole-grain flours, there are mills that offer them by mail order. Of course, the best guarantee of freshness, especially if you are a serious baker, is to grind your own grains. This is not as expensive as you might think, and if you bake frequently, a home mill is a worthwhile investment.

MORE NONDAIRY ALTERNATIVES FOR DESSERTS:
Tofu and Other Soy Products Instead of Cheese

The thought of a cheeseless cheesecake or a custard pudding made without milk and eggs may seem absurd. However, when one considers that nearly half the world's population does not use these dairy products and still has "rich" desserts, it seems obvious that there must be satisfactory alternatives.

Various soybean products are beginning to make their way into the daily American diet, and numerous cookbooks now offer creative recipes using these foods. The soybean and its many derivatives offer protein, valuable nutrients, and unsaturated fats (without cholesterol) and lecithin. Soy foods are staples in Japanese and Chinese cuisine and can be added to the American diet as nutritious alternatives to butter, milk, meat, and cheese. Our growing interest in soy-based foods may be attributed to an increasing concern for a healthier diet as well as to the rising cost of meat and dairy products. The commercial food industry has been experimenting with soybeans for many years, since manufacturers benefit economically from the low-cost soybean. Soy oil is made into margarine, lecithin is used as an emulsifier in salad dressings and baked goods, and texturized soy protein is added to ground meat and convenience foods as an extender.

As consumers, our familiarity with soy foods may be limited to tofu (soybean curd) and soy sauce, synonymous with Chinese restaurant fare. But there is a variety of soy products that can provide healthy and economical low-calorie alternatives to dairy foods. Soy milk can be used as a susbstitute for cow's milk. Although expensive when purchased from a health food store, it can easily be made at home from soybeans or soy flour. Tofu's consistency makes it a good substitute for such dairy products as sour cream, cottage cheese, and cream cheese. In desserts, tofu can be whipped and used in a pie, tart, or cheesecake filling. It can also be piped through a pastry tube as a decorative garnish instead of whipped cream or nut butter, which spares a considerable number of calories. Tofu is inexpensive and is sold in most health food stores and Chinese or Japanese groceries. Some supermarkets also carry tofu. Tofu can be made at home, but since it is readily purchased, no recipes have been included in this book. Like all legumes, soybeans contain substances that inhibit trypsin, an enzyme that digests the bean's protein, allowing it to be utilized by the body. Therefore, soybeans and products such as soy flour or soy milk must be cooked before consumption.

NUTRITIONAL YEASTS

Brewer's yeast is a by-product of the brewing process. It contains concentrated amounts of protein and other nutrients, particularly the B vitamins. Brewer's yeast should be purchased "debittered," which greatly improves its taste; this information is stated on the label.

Torula yeast is grown primarily as a food supplement. It is higher in protein and nutrients than brewer's yeast, and has an iron content. Torula is also lower in sodium than brewer's yeast. The molasses medium on which torula is grown lends a mild flavor, which does not overpower the food to which the yeast is added.

Both types of nutritional yeast are available in flake or powdered form. Unlike baker's yeast they are not alive and do not have to be refrigerated. Although both yeasts can be used in baking and desserts, torula has a less pronounced flavor and a higher nutritional value. Brewer's yeast (sometimes labeled Saccharomyces cerevisiae) has a somewhat "cheesy" flavor, which blends harmoniously with tofu for various cheesecake and pastry fillings.

FOOD COLORINGS

Added colorings are used to enhance the visual appeal of many food products. They are widely used commercially, particularly in packaged or frozen convenience foods, and any product containing either naturally derived or synthetic colorings must be labeled "artificially colored." Food colors are responsible for the aesthetic appeal of pastel rosettes on special party cakes. With a few exceptions, they serve no nutritional purpose and, except for a few naturally derived colorings (such as beta carotene and ferrous gluconate) are considered potentially dangerous. Many of the synthetic food colors were banned or restricted when they were shown to promote cancer in laboratory animals.

As consumers in a country that relies on convenience products, we have become conditioned to brightly colored foods when, in fact, these are not their true colors. Desserts can be visually enticing without the use of food colors. Spices, carob, and grain "coffee" impart their natural caramel colors, as do barley malt syrup and sorghum. A beautiful rose shade can be derived from beets or fresh cherries. Chlorophyll, a green plant pigment, can be used to tint a mint-colored filling; it is available in liquid form in some health food stores. A thread or two of saffron can be lightly cooked in a tablespoon of oil and then used as a yellow coloring for desserts. All of these natural colors can be added to almond paste or whipped tofu and used to decorate special-occasion cakes.

* * *

I have intended this to be an objective discussion of the more commonly used dessert ingredients and their alternatives. Ideally, flours would always be whole-grain and freshly milled; nuts would be cracked fresh from the shell; fruit would be organically grown and just picked. Naturally, though, compromises must be made to accommodate taste, convenience, and busy schedules, and I have tried to do this without too much nutritional sacrifice.

Initially you may wish to modify these recipes to prepare desserts more like those you are accustomed to. If you are a sugar lover and trying out the recipes for the first time, you may be happier with part or all maple syrup than with the more unfamiliar flavors of grain-syrup sweeteners. The same holds true for flours; until you become accustomed to the taste and texture of pure whole grains you may prefer to mix whole-grain flours with unbleached white or whole wheat pastry flour. But you will be pleasantly surprised at how readily your palate adapts and at how easy and satisfying it can be to serve healthful, delicious, and beautiful desserts.

Cookies

LEMON–TOFU FANCIES
DATE OR FIG PINWHEEL COOKIES
GINGERSNAPS
GINGERBREAD MEN
REFRIGERATOR GINGERSNAPS
LINZER COOKIES
MOLASSES SNAPS
ORANGE–PECAN CRISPS
CRUNCHY SPICE COOKIES
CINNAMON GRAHAM CRACKERS

Oatmeal raisin cookies, peanut butter cookies, brownies, gingerbread men! Cookies are everybody's favorite snack. Whose childhood didn't include the after-school ritual of cookies and ice-cold milk? As adults we might forgo the milk, but who of us can resist a plate piled high with our favorite cookies? What better place to begin a conversion from traditional desserts. You'll be surprised by the lightness and good taste of the assortment offered here. Cookies are fun to make and great to have on hand. Isn't it nice to know that they can be nutritious too?

For perfect results, keep these things in mind:

- Cookies should be baked on shiny baking sheets; those with darkened surfaces cause cookies to brown too quickly.
- Use rimless baking sheets for even browning and heat circulation.
- Most cookie doughs or batters should be handled as little as possible. Overbeating or kneading will make cookies tough.
- Grease baking sheets with vegetable oil, margarine, or liquid lecithin (lecithin may need to be warmed slightly for easy spreading).
- Cookies should be removed with a metal spatula while still hot; let cool on wire racks.
- Store crisp cookies in a container with the cover ajar, or loosely cover container with waxed paper. Soft cookies should be stored in an airtight container.
- Some cookie doughs can be used to make pie or tart pastry (see Pies, Tarts, and Puff Pastry, page 55).
- Experiment with natural flavorings and spices, such as cinnamon, nutmeg, allspice, cloves, ground nuts, and finely grated orange or lemon peel. Various liquids—fruit juices, herb teas, grain coffee substitute—are interchangeable as well.
- Cookies made with liquid sweeteners, carob powder, or soy flour tend to brown quickly. Check frequently to avoid overbaking.

- For best results preheat the oven for at least 15 minutes.
- Never overcrowd the oven with baking sheets. If you use two oven racks, switch baking sheets midway during baking so that the cookies brown evenly.
- Since these cookies contain no leavening, they will not expand during baking. Therefore you may wish to make them a bit larger than you would with leavened dough.

❖ BASIC COOKIE DOUGH ❖

When time is limited, try this recipe to satisfy a sweet tooth.

MAKES 3 TO 4 DOZEN

½ cup corn or safflower oil
½ cup natural liquid sweetener
¼ cup liquid (unfiltered apple or other unsweetened fruit juice, grain coffee substitute, decaffeinated coffee, or herb tea)
1 teaspoon vanilla extract
1¼ (or more) cups whole wheat pastry flour
¼ teaspoon salt (optional)
Optional flavorings: 1 teaspoon ground cinnamon; pinch of freshly grated nutmeg; grated peel of 1 orange or lemon (use juice as liquid in recipe); ½ cup finely chopped walnuts or pecans; or ¾ cup ground almonds (decrease oil to 1½ tablespoons)

Preheat oven to 350° F. Grease baking sheets. Combine liquid ingredients in food processor fitted with steel blade or in mixing bowl and blend well. Add flour, salt, and optional flavoring and blend just until dough begins to form ball; do not overblend or cookies will be tough. Dough should be soft but not sticky; add more flour by tablespoonfuls if dough is too soft.

For drop cookies: Drop dough by rounded tablespoonfuls onto prepared baking sheets.

For ball cookies: Roll dough into 1-inch balls. Arrange 1 inch apart on prepared baking sheets.

For refrigerator cookies: Form dough into 2-inch cylinder. Wrap in foil or plastic wrap and refrigerate overnight. Cut dough into ¼-inch-thick slices. Arrange 1 inch apart on prepared baking sheets.

Bake until edges of cookies are lightly browned, about 10 to 15 minutes depending on shaping technique. Transfer to racks to cool.

❖ *ALMOND CRESCENT COOKIES* ❖

MAKES 2½ TO 3 DOZEN

---

    1 cup (2 sticks) margarine
    ½ cup natural liquid sweetener
    1 teaspoon vanilla extract or ¼ teaspoon almond extract
    1¾ cups whole wheat pastry flour
    1 cup finely ground almonds
       Grated peel of 1 lemon (optional)

       Maple syrup and finely ground almonds (optional)

Preheat oven to 350°F. Lightly grease baking sheets. Combine margarine, sweetener, and flavoring extract in food processor fitted with steel blade or in mixing bowl and blend well. In separate bowl combine flour, almonds, and lemon peel. Add to margarine mixture and blend just until dry ingredients are moistened (dough will be sticky). Roll dough into 1-inch balls with floured hands. Arrange 1 inch apart on prepared baking sheets. Flatten slightly with palm and shape into crescents. Bake until edges are lightly browned, about 15 to 17 minutes. Transfer to racks to cool.

When completely cool, lightly brush cookies with maple syrup if desired; sprinkle with ground almonds.

❖ *CHINESE ALMOND COOKIES* ❖

MAKES ABOUT 2½ DOZEN

---

    1 cup (2 sticks) margarine or ¾ cup corn oil
    ½ cup natural liquid sweetener (preferably rice syrup)
    ¼ teaspoon almond extract
    2 cups whole wheat pastry flour
    ½ cup finely ground almonds
    ¼ cup millet or rice flour
    1 tablespoon arrowroot
       Halved or slivered almonds

Preheat oven to 325°F. Grease baking sheets. Combine margarine, sweetener, and almond extract in food processor fitted with steel blade or in mixing bowl and blend well. In separate bowl combine whole wheat flour, ground almonds, millet or rice flour and arrowroot. Add to margarine mixture and blend just until dry ingredients are moistened. Roll dough into 1-inch balls. Arrange 2 inches apart on prepared baking sheets. Flatten slightly with palm. Press halved or slivered almond into center of each cookie. Bake until golden, about 12 to 15 minutes. Transfer to racks to cool.

❖ *LEMON–ALMOND COOKIES* ❖

A chewy, delicate tea cookie with a tangy lemon flavor.

MAKES ABOUT 1½ DOZEN

½ cup corn oil
½ cup natural liquid sweetener
1½ tablespoons fresh lemon juice
1 cup finely ground blanched almonds, toasted
1 cup whole wheat pastry flour
½ teaspoon grated lemon peel
Halved or slivered almonds (optional)

Preheat oven to 350°F. Grease baking sheets. Combine oil, sweetener, and lemon juice in food processor fitted with steel blade or in mixing bowl and blend well. In separate bowl combine ground almonds, flour, and lemon peel. Add to oil mixture and blend just until dry ingredients are moistened (dough will be sticky). Roll dough into 1-inch balls with floured hands. Arrange 2 inches apart on prepared baking sheets. Press halved or slivered almond into center of each cookie if desired. Bake until golden, about 10 to 12 minutes. Transfer to racks to cool.

❖ *CAROB CHIP COOKIES* ❖

MAKES ABOUT 2 DOZEN

½ cup corn oil
½ cup natural liquid sweetener
¼ cup powdered grain coffee substitute or decaffeinated
coffee
1½ teaspoons vanilla extract
1½ cups whole wheat pastry flour
1 teaspoon arrowroot or 2 teaspoons nut butter
1 teaspoon ground cinnamon
12 ounces unsweetened carob chips (see note)
½ cup chopped pecans or walnuts (optional)

Preheat oven to 325°F. Grease baking sheets. Combine oil, sweetener, coffee, and vanilla (and nut butter, if using) in food processor fitted with steel blade or in mixing bowl and blend well. In separate bowl combine flour, arrowroot, and cinnamon. Add to oil mixture and blend just until dry ingredients are moistened. Transfer dough to bowl and stir in carob chips and nuts (if desired). Drop by rounded tablespoonfuls onto prepared baking sheets, spacing 2 inches apart. Bake until golden, about 10 to 12 minutes. Transfer to racks to cool.

NOTE: *Check package carefully; most carob chips are sweetened, but there are unsweetened brands available. Carob chips are made with nonfat dry milk and therefore are not for those on dairy-free diets.*

❖ *FIG* OR *DATE COOKIES* ❖

MAKES ABOUT 2 DOZEN

¾ cup (1½ sticks) margarine
¼ cup natural liquid sweetener
1 teaspoon vanilla extract
2 cups whole wheat pastry flour
1 cup soaked, drained, and finely chopped dried figs or 1
cup finely chopped pitted dates
¾ cup chopped nuts

Preheat oven to 325°F. Grease baking sheets. Combine margarine, sweetener, and vanilla in food processor fitted with steel blade or in mixing bowl and blend well. Add flour, fruit, and nuts and blend just until all ingredients are moistened. Drop by rounded tablespoonfuls onto prepared baking sheets, spacing 2 inches apart. Bake until golden, about 25 minutes. Transfer to racks to cool.

•:• OATMEAL–CAROB COOKIES •:•

MAKES ABOUT 2 DOZEN

¾ cup corn oil
½ cup natural liquid sweetener
¼ cup unsweetened carob powder
¼ cup powdered grain coffee substitute or decaffeinated coffee
1½ teaspoons vanilla extract
¾ cup whole wheat pastry flour
1 teaspoon ground cinnamon
¼ teaspoon salt

2 cups rolled oats
½ cup chopped pecans or walnuts (optional)

Preheat oven to 350°F. Generously grease baking sheets. Combine oil, sweetener, carob powder, coffee, and vanilla in food processor fitted with steel blade or in mixing bowl and blend well. In separate bowl combine flour, cinnamon, and salt. Add to oil mixture and blend just until dry ingredients are moistened.

Transfer to large mixing bowl and stir in oats and nuts. Drop by rounded tablespoonfuls onto prepared baking sheets, spacing 2 inches apart. Bake until golden, about 12 to 15 minutes. Transfer to racks to cool.

❖ *OATMEAL–ORANGE COOKIES* ❖

MAKES ABOUT 1½ DOZEN

½ cup corn oil
½ cup natural liquid sweetener
3 tablespoons fresh or reconstituted frozen unsweetened orange juice
1 tablespoon nut butter or liquid lecithin
1 teaspoon vanilla extract
½ cup oat flour
½ cup whole wheat pastry flour
1 tablespoon nutritional yeast flakes
Grated peel of orange
¼ teaspoon salt (optional)

2½ cups rolled oats

Preheat oven to 350°F. Generously grease baking sheets. Combine oil, sweetener, juice, nut butter or lecithin, and vanilla in food processor fitted with steel blade or in mixing bowl and blend well. In separate bowl combine flours, yeast flakes, orange peel, salt. Add to oil mixture and blend just until dry ingredients are moistened.

Transfer to large mixing bowl and stir in oats. Drop by rounded table-spoonfuls onto prepared baking sheets, spacing 2 inches apart. Bake until golden, about 12 to 15 minutes. Transfer to racks to cool.

❖ OATMEAL–RAISIN COOKIES ❖

MAKES ABOUT 2 DOZEN

¾ cup corn oil
¾ cup natural liquid sweetener
¼ cup unfiltered apple juice or water
1 tablespoon nut butter or liquid lecithin
1 teaspoon vanilla extract
¾ cup whole wheat pastry flour
2 tablespoons nutritional yeast flakes
1 teaspoon ground cinnamon
¼ teaspoon salt (optional)

2¾ cups rolled oats
½ cup raisins (see note)
½ cup chopped pecans

Preheat oven to 350°F. Generously grease baking sheets. Combine oil, sweetener, juice, nut butter or lecithin, and vanilla in food processor fitted with steel blade or in mixing bowl and blend well. In separate bowl combine flour, yeast flakes, cinnamon, and salt. Add to oil mixture and blend just until dry ingredients are moistened.

Transfer to large mixing bowl and stir in oats, raisins, and pecans. Drop by rounded tablespoonfuls onto prepared baking sheets, spacing 2 inches apart. Bake until golden, about 15 to 17 minutes. Transfer to racks to cool.

NOTE: *If raisins are very dry, soak 15 minutes in required liquid and vanilla. Drain off liquid and use in recipe.*

❖ *PEANUTTY OATMEAL COOKIES* ❖

MAKES ABOUT 6 DOZEN

¾ cup natural liquid sweetener
½ cup corn oil
¼ cup soy milk
⅓ cup unsweetened carob powder, lightly toasted (see note, p. 64)
½ cup plus 2 tablespoons unsweetened, unsalted peanut butter
1 teaspoon vanilla extract
2¾ cups rolled oats

Preheat oven to 325°F. Generously grease baking sheets. Combine sweetener, oil, soy milk, and carob powder in large heavy saucepan. Bring to simmer over medium heat; let simmer, stirring until well blended, 3 to 5 minutes. Remove from heat and blend in peanut butter and vanilla. Stir in oats. Drop by rounded tablespoonfuls onto prepared baking sheets. Bake until golden, about 8 to 10 minutes, checking frequently to be sure that edges do not brown too quickly. Transfer to racks to cool.

❖ *PEANUT BUTTER COOKIES* ❖

MAKES ABOUT 2 DOZEN

½ cup unsweetened, unsalted peanut butter (preferably crunchy-style)
½ cup (1 stick) margarine
½ cup natural liquid sweetener
1 tablespoon water
1 teaspoon vanilla extract
1½ cups whole wheat pastry flour

Preheat oven to 350°F. Grease baking sheets. Combine peanut butter, margarine, sweetener, water, and vanilla in food processor fitted with steel blade or in mixing bowl and blend well. Add flour and mix until dough forms soft ball. Roll dough into 1-inch balls. Arrange 2 inches apart on prepared baking sheets. Flatten each ball with floured fork, pressing once vertically and once horizontally to form crosshatch design. Bake until edges are browned, about 12 to 15 minutes. Transfer to racks to cool.

❖ MEXICAN WALNUT COOKIES ❖

MAKES 4 TO 5 DOZEN

¾ cup corn oil
¾ cup natural liquid sweetener
1 teaspoon vanilla extract
4 cups whole wheat pastry flour or 2 cups whole wheat
   pastry flour, 1½ cups unbleached all-purpose flour, and
   1½ cups brown rice flour
2 cups finely chopped walnuts
1 teaspoon ground cinnamon
½ teaspoon arrowroot

Preheat oven to 350°F. Combine oil, sweetener, and vanilla in food processor fitted with steel blade or in mixing bowl and blend well. In separate bowl combine flour, nuts, cinnamon, and arrowroot. Add to oil mixture and blend just until dry ingredients are moistened. Roll dough into 1-inch balls. Arrange 1 inch apart on greased baking sheets. Flatten centers slightly with thumb. Bake until golden, about 10 to 12 minutes. Transfer to racks to cool.

❖ *NO-BAKE CAROB FUDGE COOKIES* ❖

MAKES ABOUT 4 DOZEN

½ to ¾ cup natural liquid sweetener
   ½ cup soy milk
   ¼ cup corn oil
   ⅓ cup unsweetened carob powder
   ¼ cup unsweetened, unsalted peanut butter
 1½ cups rolled oats

Combine sweetener, soy milk, oil, and carob in medium-size saucepan and bring to boil. Let boil 1 minute, then remove from heat. Blend in peanut butter. Add oats and stir until evenly moistened. Drop mixture by tablespoonfuls onto waxed paper and let cool. Store airtight.

❖ *NO-BAKE COCONUT MACAROONS* ❖

MAKES ABOUT 2 DOZEN

1¾ cups shredded unsweetened coconut
  ½ cup natural liquid sweetener
  3 tablespoons soy milk
  2 tablespoons arrowroot
    Pinch of salt (optional)
  ¼ cup Flaxseed Whip (page 168)

Combine coconut, sweetener, soy milk, arrowroot, and salt in medium-size heavy saucepan. Place over medium-high heat and bring to boil, then reduce heat and simmer 3 minutes. Let mixture cool. Fold in flaxseed whip. Drop by tablespoonfuls onto lightly greased waxed paper or parchment paper. Transfer to airtight container and refrigerate.

VARIATIONS:

Carob Macaroons: Add ¼ cup lightly toasted unsweetened carob powder (see note, p. 64) to coconut mixture before cooking.

Almond Macaroons: Fold in ½ cup finely chopped toasted almonds along with flaxseed whip, *or* blend ½ cup Frangipane Filling (page 90) into cooked mixture before folding in flaxseed whip.

Honey Macaroons: Use ¼ cup honey for half of the natural liquid sweetener called for in the recipe.

Fruit Macaroons: Make indentation in center of each macaroon with teaspoon. Fill with fruit preserves of your choice.

❖ NO-BAKE WALNUT OR PECAN KISSES ❖

MAKES ABOUT 2 DOZEN

---

2 cups ground walnuts or pecans
¼ cup maple syrup or other natural liquid sweetener
2 tablespoons powdered grain coffee substitute
Unsweetened carob powder, lightly toasted (see note, p. 64)

Combine nuts, sweetener, and coffee in food processor fitted with steel blade and blend well. Chill mixture 1 hour. Roll into 1-inch balls. Roll balls in carob powder to coat evenly. Store airtight in cool area.

❖ APRICOT SQUARES ❖

MAKES ABOUT THIRTY 2-INCH SQUARES

FILLING:
½ cup chopped unsulfured dried apricots
½ cup natural liquid sweetener

DOUGH:
½ cup corn oil
½ cup natural liquid sweetener
1¼ cups whole wheat pastry flour
½ cup cooked millet, well drained
½ cup rolled oats
1 teaspoon ground cinnamon

For filling: Combine apricots and sweetener in small saucepan and simmer until apricots are tender. Drain, reserving liquid. Let apricots cool.

For dough: Combine oil and sweetener in food processor fitted with steel blade or in mixing bowl and blend well. Add all remaining ingredients and blend until mixture forms ball, adding up to ¼ cup reserved apricot liquid if dough is too dry.

Preheat oven to 350°F. Grease 13-by-9-inch pan. Pat dough evenly into prepared pan. Spread apricots onto dough. Bake until pastry is firm, about 30 minutes. Let cool in pan, then cut into squares.

VARIATIONS:

Reduce dried fruit to ⅔ cup and add 2 tablespoons unsweetened apricot, peach, or berry puree to fruit mixture.

❖ *DRIED FRUIT AND OAT BARS* ❖

MAKES THIRTY-TWO 1-BY-2-INCH BARS

CRUST:
- 1 cup rolled oats
- ¼ cup natural liquid sweetener
- 3 tablespoons whole wheat flour
- 3 tablespoons softened margarine or corn oil

TOPPING:
- ¾ cup chopped mixed unsulfured dried fruit
- 6 tablespoons water
- 5 tablespoons natural liquid sweetener
- 1 tablespoon vegetable or soy margarine
- ¼ cup whole wheat flour
- ¼ cup finely chopped pecans or walnuts
- 3 tablespoons wheat germ
- 1 tablespoon nutritional yeast flakes
- 1 teaspoon ground cinnamon
- ¼ teaspoon allspice

Preheat oven to 350°F. Grease 8-inch square pan.

For crust: Combine oats, sweetener, flour, and margarine in medium bowl and blend well. Pat evenly into prepared pan. Bake 7 minutes.

For topping: While crust is baking, combine dried fruit, water, sweetener, and margarine in medium saucepan and bring to boil. Remove from heat and let cool slightly. Stir in all remaining ingredients. Spread mixture over baked crust. Bake until topping is set, about 25 minutes. Let cool, then cut into bars.

❖ CAROB–NUT BROWNIES ❖

MAKES SIXTEEN 2-INCH SQUARES

⅔ cup natural liquid sweetener
½ cup corn oil
⅓ cup soy milk
1 tablespoon liquid lecithin
1 teaspoon vanilla extract
1 cup whole wheat pastry flour
⅓ cup unsweetened carob powder, lightly toasted (see note, p. 64)
2 teaspoons oat or soy flour
½ teaspoon ground cinnamon
½ teaspoon salt (optional)
½ to ¾ cup chopped pecans or walnuts

Preheat oven to 325°F. Combine sweetener, oil, soy milk, lecithin, and vanilla in food processor fitted with steel blade or in mixing bowl and blend well. In separate bowl combine whole wheat flour, carob, oat or soy flour, cinnamon, and salt. Add to oil mixture and stir (do not beat) just until all ingredients are evenly moistened. Stir in nuts. Spread mixture in ungreased 8-inch square pan. Bake until firm, about 25 to 30 minutes. Let cool in pan, then cut into squares.

❖ *CAROB BROWNIES* ❖

These could sway even the most ardent chocolate lover. Lightly toasted carob powder, combined with the subtle flavors of banana and coffee, results in a rich, moist brownie.

12 SMALL SERVINGS

½ cup corn oil
5 tablespoons natural liquid sweetener
3 tablespoons unsweetened carob powder, lightly toasted (see note, p. 64)
1 medium-size ripe banana, peeled
⅓ cup powdered grain coffee substitute or decaffeinated coffee
1 teaspoon vanilla extract
1¼ cups whole wheat pastry flour
1 teaspoon baking powder
½ teaspoon ground cinnamon (optional)
¼ teaspoon salt
½ cup chopped nuts (optional)

Preheat oven to 350°F. Grease 8-inch square pan. Combine oil and sweetener in food processor or large bowl of electric mixer and blend until syrupy. Break banana into several pieces (mash if using electric mixer), add to oil mixture, and blend well. Mix in coffee and vanilla. Sift together dry ingredients and add all at once, beating just until blended; do not overbeat. Turn batter into prepared pan. Sprinkle with nuts if desired. Bake until tester inserted near center comes out clean, about 40 minutes; if brownies seem too moist even when tester is clean, leave pan in oven with heat turned off for a few more minutes. Let pan cool on rack 15 minutes. Cut brownies while still warm but not hot.

VARIATIONS:

Split individual squares in half and fill with thin layer of Tofu-Almond Creme (page 136), or Creamy Tofu Cheese Filling (page 175) flavored with powdered grain coffee substitute.

❖ *COCONUT–RASPBERRY SQUARES* ❖

MAKES ABOUT 2 DOZEN SMALL SQUARES

1 recipe Basic Cookie Dough (page 25)
  Grated peel of 1 lemon

1¾ cups shredded unsweetened coconut
⅓ cup natural liquid sweetener
2 tablespoons almond butter
2 tablespoons soy milk
¾ cup raspberry preserves

Prepare cookie dough, flavoring with lemon peel. Wrap and chill thoroughly.

Preheat oven to 350°F. Grease 8-inch square pan. Combine coconut, sweetener, almond butter, and soy milk in medium-size saucepan and place over low heat until heated through, stirring to blend; do not boil. Remove from heat and let cool to lukewarm. Meanwhile, pat cookie dough evenly into prepared pan. Spread with raspberry preserves. Top with coconut mixture. Bake until golden, about 12 to 15 minutes. Let cool in pan, then cut into small squares.

❖ *LEMON ZEST–ALMOND BARS* ❖

These delicately textured cookies will give your palate a twang. They become even zestier if stored airtight for a few days.

MAKES APPROXIMATELY 16 2¼" SQUARES

CRUST:

1½ cups whole wheat pastry flour
½ cup finely ground almonds
½ teaspoon arrowroot
¼ teaspoon salt (optional)
1½ tablespoons natural liquid sweetener
1 teaspoon vanilla extract
½ teaspoon grated lemon peel
10 tablespoons (1¼ sticks) margarine or ½ cup (1 stick) margarine plus 2 tablespoons corn oil, all well chilled
3 to 4 tablespoons ice water

TOPPING:

½ cup soy milk
¼ cup natural liquid sweetener
2 tablespoons fresh lemon juice
2 tablespoons margarine or 1½ tablespoons corn oil
1 teaspoon arrowroot
½ teaspoon grated lemon peel

3 tablespoons chopped blanched almonds

For crust: Lightly grease 9-inch square pan. Combine flour, almonds, arrowroot, and salt in food processor fitted with steel blade or in mixing bowl and blend briefly. Drizzle in sweetener and vanilla. Sprinkle in lemon peel. Cut margarine into 1-inch pieces and blend in (along with oil, if using) just until mixture resembles coarse crumbs. Sprinkle in ice water 1 tablespoonful at a time, adding only enough to make mixture hold together. Pat dough into prepared pan, spreading evenly. Chill at least 1 hour.

Preheat oven to 400°F. Prick crust all over with fork. Bake until lightly golden, about 10 minutes. Let cool.

Meanwhile, prepare topping: Reduce oven temperature to 350°F. Combine soy milk, sweetener, lemon juice, margarine or oil, arrowroot, and lemon peel in small saucepan and bring to boil. Simmer until mixture just begins to thicken. Remove from heat and let cool to lukewarm. Spread onto crust. Sprinkle with chopped almonds. Bake until topping is firm, about 10 to 12 minutes. Let cool, then cut into squares or bars. Store airtight at least 2 days for best flavor.

❖ *SUNFLOWER–RAISIN SQUARES* ❖

MAKES ABOUT THIRTY 2-INCH SQUARES

---

  1 cup raisins
¾ cup unfiltered apple juice
½ cup corn oil
¼ cup natural liquid sweetener
  2 tablespoons nut butter

1½ cups whole wheat pastry flour
  1 teaspoon ground cinnamon
½ teaspoon freshly grated nutmeg
¼ teaspoon ground cloves
½ cup hulled unsalted sunflower seeds

Combine raisins and apple juice in large saucepan and simmer until raisins are soft. Remove from heat and stir in oil. Let cool to lukewarm, then blend in sweetener and nut butter.

Preheat oven to 350°F. Grease 13-by-9 inch pan. Combine flour and spices in medium-size bowl. Add to raisin mixture along with sunflower seeds and stir until all ingredients are evenly moistened. Spread dough in prepared pan. Bake until firm, about 15 to 20 minutes. Let pan cool on rack, then cut into squares.

❖ *FILLED BAR COOKIES* ❖

*This is one of my favorite cookie recipes. I think the bars are partic-
ularly good with a moist fig filling, but they are also delicious made
with other fruit preserves.*

MAKES ABOUT 3 DOZEN

---

  1 cup (2 sticks) vegetable or soy margarine
  ½ cup natural liquid sweetener
2½ cups whole wheat flour
  1 cup whole wheat pastry flour
  1 teaspoon ground cinnamon
  ½ teaspoon salt (optional)
  1 recipe fig Dried Fruit Filling (page 152) or any Fruit
     Filling (page 169)

Combine margarine, sweetener, and maple syrup in food processor fitted
with steel blade or in mixing bowl and blend well. In separate bowl
combine flours, cinnamon, and salt. Add to margarine mixture and
blend just until dough begins to form ball. Transfer dough to lightly
floured surface and knead gently 1 minute. Divide in half and form into
two 2-inch cylinders. Wrap in foil or plastic wrap and refrigerate at least
3 hours or overnight.

Preheat oven to 325°F. Generously grease baking sheets. On lightly
floured surface, roll each cylinder out into long 2-inch-wide strip. Spoon
filling in narrow stripe down center of dough. Bring long edges of dough
together and pinch to seal. Transfer to prepared baking sheets and bake
until golden, about 15 to 17 minutes. Let baking sheet cool on rack, then
cut into 2-inch bars. Store airtight, placing piece of fresh bread or orange
peel in container to keep bars moist.

❖ FILLED COOKIES ❖

MAKES ABOUT 2½ DOZEN

1 recipe Basic Cookie Dough (page 25) or variation
¾ cup Dried Fruit Filling (page 169) or any Fruit Filling
(page 152)

Prepare cookie dough, wrap, and chill.

Preheat oven to 350°F. Grease baking sheets. On lightly floured surface, roll dough out to thickness of ¼ inch. Cut into desired shapes with cookie cutters. Cut out centers of half of cookies with smaller cutters or thimble. Transfer solid cookies to prepared baking sheets. Spread each with ½ teaspoon filling. Top with cutout cookie. Seal edges with fork. Bake until lightly golden, about 12 to 15 minutes. Transfer to racks to cool.

❖ POPPYSEED–POTATO COOKIES ❖

A great way to use leftover mashed potatoes!

MAKES ABOUT 3 DOZEN

1 cup mashed potatoes
¾ cup (1½ sticks) margarine
⅓ cup natural liquid sweetener
1 cup whole wheat pastry flour
¼ cup finely chopped nuts
1 tablespoon poppyseeds
1 teaspoon arrowroot
½ teaspoon ground cinnamon

Combine potatoes, margarine, and sweetener in large saucepan and place over medium-low heat until heated through, stirring to blend. Remove from heat and let cool to lukewarm. In bowl combine all remaining ingredients. Stir into potato mixture to form soft dough. Wrap in foil or plastic wrap and chill at least 2 hours. *(recipe continues)*

Preheat oven to 350°F. Lightly grease baking sheets. On lightly floured surface roll dough out to thickness of ¼ inch. Cut into desired shapes with cookie cutters. Arrange on prepared baking sheets. Bake until golden, about 15 to 18 minutes. Transfer to racks to cool.

VARIATIONS:

Dough can also be rolled into 1-inch balls without chilling. Arrange on prepared baking sheets and flatten slightly with fork. Bake as directed.

Carob–Poppyseed–Potato Cookies: Add 1 tablespoon lightly toasted unsweetened carob powder (see note, p. 64) to cooked mixture. Top with Carob Glaze (page 128).

Lemon–Poppyseed–Potato Cookies: Add 1 teaspoon grated lemon peel and 1 teaspoon fresh lemon juice to cooked mixture. Top with Lemon-Maple Glaze (page 179).

Raisin–Poppyseed–Potato Cookies: Add ½ cup raisins (lightly dredged in flour) and 1 teaspoon vanilla to cooked mixture.

•:• SCOTCH SHORTBREAD •:•

A rich cookie that is very quick to prepare. Stored airtight, these actually improve with age.

MAKES ABOUT 2 DOZEN WEDGES

---

1 cup (2 sticks) margarine
½ cup plus 2 tablespoons natural liquid sweetener
2 to 2¼ cups whole wheat pastry flour
1 teaspoon arrowroot

Preheat oven to 325°F. Combine margarine and sweetener in food processor fitted with steel blade or in mixing bowl and blend well. Add 2 cups flour along with arrowroot and blend until mixture forms soft ball, adding remaining flour by tablespoonfuls if dough is too soft. Pat evenly into 8-inch flan ring, tart pan, or shortbread mold. Prick all over with fork. Bake until golden, about 15 minutes. Cut into wedges while warm.

VARIATIONS:

Carob Shortbread: Add ¼ cup unsweetened carob powder to flour mixture.

Lemon or Orange Shortbread: Add grated peel of 1 lemon or orange to flour mixture.

Nut Shortbread: Add ½ cup finely chopped almonds, pecans, or walnuts to flour mixture.

Spice Shortbread: Add 1½ teaspoons ground cinnamon and a pinch of freshly grated nutmeg to flour mixture.

•:• *SWEDISH RAGALACH* •:•

A traditional Christmas cookie in many Swedish households.

MAKES 8 DOZEN

DOUGH:
- ¾ cup (1½ sticks) margarine
- 3 tablespoons natural liquid sweetener
- 1 tablespoon fresh lemon or orange juice
- 2 cups whole wheat pastry flour

FILLING:
- ¾ finely chopped nuts (mixture of pecans, walnuts, and almonds)
- ⅓ cup natural sweetener or unsweetened fruit preserves
- 1½ teaspoons ground cinnamon

For dough: Combine margarine, sweetener, and juice in food processor fitted with steel blade or in mixing bowl and blend well. Add flour and blend until dough forms ball. Wrap in foil or plastic wrap and chill at least 2 hours or overnight.

For filling: Combine all ingredients and blend well.

Preheat oven to 350°F. Lightly grease baking sheets. Divide dough into twelve equal parts. Shape each part into ball and roll out on lightly floured surface into 6-inch-circles. Cut each circle into eight wedges. Place ¼ teaspoon filling in center of each wedge. Roll up wedges starting from wide end. Shape into crescents. Arrange on prepared baking sheets. Bake until golden, about 10 to 12 minutes. Transfer to racks to cool.

❖ *SPRITZ COOKIES* ❖

This rich dough is traditionally shaped into Christmas trees, bells, stars, and other holiday favorites. The variations on Basic Cookie Dough (page 25) can be used in this recipe as well.

MAKES ABOUT 2½ DOZEN

1 cup (2 sticks) margarine
½ cup natural liquid sweetener
2 tablespoons almond butter
2½ cups whole wheat pastry flour
　　Pinch of salt (optional)
　　Date sugar and ground cinnamon for topping (optional)
　　Natural liquid sweetener for glaze (optional)

Preheat oven to 350°F. Grease baking sheets. Combine margarine, sweetener, and almond butter in food processor fitted with steel blade or in mixing bowl and blend well. Add flour and salt and blend just until dough begins to form ball. Transfer to lightly floured surface and knead gently 2 minutes. Spoon dough into pastry bag or spritz gun. Form desired shapes on prepared baking sheets. sprinkle with date sugar and cinnamon if desired. Bake until firm and lightly golden, about 8 to 10 minutes. Brush warm cookies with sweetener to glaze if desired. Transfer to racks to cool.

Dough can also be divided in half, wrapped in foil or plastic wrap, and chilled thoroughly. Roll out on lightly floured surface to thickness of ¼ inch. Cut into desired shapes with cookie cutters. Arrange on prepared baking sheets and bake as directed.

❖ LEMON–TOFU FANCIES ❖

MAKES ABOUT 3 DOZEN

¾ cup (1½ sticks) margarine
¾ cup natural liquid sweetener
⅓ cup soft tofu
2 tablespoons almond butter
2 tablespoons fresh lemon juice
1 tablespoon liquid lecithin
1½ teaspoons grated lemon peel
2½ to 2¾ cups whole wheat pastry flour
Lemon-Maple Glaze (page 179)
Finely chopped pistachios

Preheat oven to 350°F. Grease baking sheets. Combine margarine, sweetener, tofu, almond butter, lemon juice, lecithin, and lemon peel in food processor fitted with steel blade or in mixing bowl and blend well. Add 2½ cups flour and blend just until dough forms ball, adding more if dough is too soft. Spoon dough into pastry bag or spritz gun. Form strips, wreaths, or pretzel shapes on prepared baking sheets. Bake until lightly golden, about 10 to 12 minutes. Dip end of each warm cookie into lemon-maple glaze, then into pistachios. Transfer to racks to cool.

❖ DATE OR FIG PINWHEEL COOKIES ❖

MAKES 3 TO 4 DOZEN

½ cup (1 stick) margarine
½ cup natural liquid sweetener
1 tablespoon cold water or grain coffee substitute or decaffeinated coffee, chilled
1 teaspoon vanilla extract
1½ cups whole wheat pastry flour
⅛ teaspoon salt (optional)
1 recipe date or fig Dried Fruit Filling (page 169)

Combine margarine, sweetener, water, and vanilla in food processor fitted with steel blade or in mixing bowl and blend well. Add flour and salt and blend only until dough forms ball. Divide in half. On lightly floured waxed paper, roll each half out into 12-by-16-inch rectangle. Spread evenly with filling. Roll up from long side, pinching edge to seal. Wrap rolls in foil or plastic wrap and chill at least 3 hours.

Preheat oven to 350°F. Lightly grease baking sheets. Cut rolls into ¼-inch-thick slices. Arrange 1 inch apart on prepared baking sheets. Bake until golden, about 10 to 12 minutes. Transfer to racks to cool.

❖ *GINGERSNAPS* ❖

MAKES ABOUT 4 DOZEN

¾ cup natural liquid sweetener
½ cup corn or safflower oil
¼ cup blackstrap molasses
2¾ cups whole wheat pastry flour
1 teaspoon ground ginger
1 teaspoon arrowroot
½ teaspoon ground cinnamon
½ teaspoon salt
¼ teaspoon ground cloves

Combine sweetener, oil, and molasses in large saucepan and heat through, stirring to blend. Remove from heat and let cool. Blend in all remaining ingredients. Wrap dough in foil or plastic wrap and chill thoroughly.

Preheat oven to 350°F. Grease baking sheets. Divide dough into four portions. Roll out one portion at a time between sheets of greased waxed paper to ¼-inch thickness. Cut into rounds using 2-inch cutter. Arrange on prepared baking sheets. Bake until lightly browned, about 15 minutes. Immediately transfer to racks to cool.

VARIATION:

Cookies can be rolled around wooden spoon handle while still hot. Let cool completely, then serve plain or fill with Tofu Whip (page 175).

❖ GINGERBREAD MEN ❖

MAKES 1½ TO 2 DOZEN

½ cup natural liquid sweetener
¼ cup blackstrap molasses
3 tablespoons margarine
1 tablespoon corn oil
1 tablespoon soy milk
2 cups plus 2 tablespoons whole wheat pastry flour
1 teaspoon ground cinnamon
1 teaspoon ground ginger
½ teaspoon allspice
½ teaspoon arrowroot
¼ teaspoon salt (optional)

Chopped nuts and/or unsweetened carob chips
(optional garnishes)

Combine sweetener, molasses, margarine, oil, and soy milk in large saucepan and stir over low heat until margarine is melted. Cool to lukewarm. In bowl combine flour, spices, arrowroot, and salt. Stir into molasses mixture. Wrap dough in foil or plastic wrap and chill thoroughly.

Preheat oven to 350°F. Generously grease baking sheets. On lightly floured surface, roll dough out to ¼-inch thickness. Cut with gingerbread man or other cutters. Arrange on prepared baking sheets. Decorate with nuts and carob chips if desired. Bake until golden, about 10 to 12 minutes. Transfer to racks to cool.

❖ *REFRIGERATOR GINGERSNAPS* ❖

MAKES 2½ TO 3 DOZEN

½ cup corn oil
½ cup natural liquid sweetener
⅓ cup soy milk
¼ cup blackstrap molasses
1 teaspoon powdered grain coffee substitute or decaffeinated coffee
2¼ cups (or more) whole wheat pastry flour
1 teaspoon ground ginger
½ teaspoon ground cinnamon
¼ teaspoon ground cloves
¼ teaspoon salt (optional)

Natural liquid sweetener or maple syrup (optional)

Combine oil and sweetener in food processor fitted with steel blade or in mixing bowl and cream well. Add soy milk, molasses, and coffee and blend. In separate bowl combine 2¼ cups flour, spices, and salt. Add to oil mixture and blend just until soft dough forms, adding more flour by tablespoonfuls if dough is too soft to handle. Form into 2-inch cylinder. Wrap in foil or plastic wrap and chill at least 3 hours or overnight.

Preheat oven to 350°F. Grease baking sheets. Cut dough into ¼-inch-thick slices. Arrange 1 inch apart on prepared baking sheets. Bake until golden, about 12 to 15 minutes. If desired, glaze warm cookies by brushing lightly with sweetener or syrup. Transfer to racks to cool.

VARIATION:

Raisin Gingersnaps: Decrease flour to 2 cups (dough will be sticky). Add ½ cup raisins (lightly dredged in flour) and 1 teaspoon vanilla. Drop dough by tablespoonfuls onto prepared baking sheets. Bake as directed.

❖ LINZER COOKIES ❖

MAKES ABOUT 5 DOZEN

¾ cup corn oil
¾ cup natural liquid sweetener
2 teaspoons vanilla extract
3 cups whole wheat pastry flour
¼ cup unsweetened carob powder
¼ cup finely chopped pecans
1 tablespoon arrowroot
1 teaspoon grated lemon peel
1 teaspoon ground cinnamon
¼ teaspoon ground cloves
   Pinch of freshly grated nutmeg

¾ cup raspberry preserves

Combine oil, sweetener, and vanilla in food processor fitted with steel blade or in mixing bowl and blend well. In separate bowl combine all remaining ingredients except preserves. Add to oil mixture and blend just until dough forms ball (dough will be soft). Divide in half and form into two 2-inch cylinders. Wrap in foil or plastic wrap and refrigerate overnight.

Preheat oven to 325°F. Lightly grease baking sheets. Cut dough into ¼-inch-thick slices, or roll into 1-inch balls. Arrange 1 inch apart on prepared baking sheets. Flatten centers with thumb. Bake until golden, about 12 to 15 minutes. Transfer to racks to cool. Spoon dab of preserves into center of each cookie.

❖ MOLASSES SNAPS ❖

MAKES ABOUT 2 DOZEN

½ cup corn oil
½ cup natural liquid sweetener
3 tablespoons blackstrap molasses
1 teaspoon vanilla extract
1 teaspoon fresh lemon juice
½ cup whole wheat pastry flour
1½ teaspoons ground ginger
¼ teaspoon salt (optional)

Preheat oven to 325°F. Generously grease baking sheets. Combine oil, sweetener, molasses, vanilla, and lemon juice in mixing bowl and blend well. Stir in flour, ginger, and salt. Drop mixture by rounded tablespoonfuls onto prepared baking sheets, spacing at least 3 inches apart. Bake until golden, about 10 to 12 minutes. Immediately transfer to racks to cool.

VARIATION:

Cookies can be rolled around wooden spoon handle while still hot. Let cool completely, then serve plain or fill with Tofu Almond Creme (page 136) or flavored Creamy Soy Whip (page 173).

❖ ORANGE–PECAN CRISPS ❖

MAKES ABOUT 3½ DOZEN

½ cup corn oil
½ cup natural liquid sweetener
¼ cup fresh or reconstituted frozen unsweetened orange juice
Grated peel of 1 orange
2½ cups whole wheat pastry flour

Combine oil, sweetener, orange juice, and peel in food processor fitted with steel blade or in mixing bowl and blend well. Add flour and blend just until dough forms ball. Divide in half and form into two 2-inch cylinders. Wrap in foil or plastic wrap and refrigerate overnight.

Preheat oven to 350°F. Grease baking sheets. Cut dough into ¼-inch-thick slices. Arrange 1 inch apart on prepared baking sheets. Bake until lightly golden, about 8 to 10 minutes. Transfer to racks to cool.

❖ CRUNCHY SPICE COOKIES ❖

MAKES 20

1⅓ cup whole wheat pastry flour
1 teaspoon ground ginger
½ teaspoon ground cinnamon
¼ teaspoon allspice
½ teaspoon baking powder
6 tablespoons margarine
5 tablespoons natural liquid sweetener
1 teaspoon vanilla extract

GLAZE
2 tablespoons natural liquid sweetener
1 teaspoon margarine

Preheat oven to 350°F. Lightly grease 8- or 9-inch square pan. Combine dry ingredients in mixing bowl and stir with a fork to mix. In medium-size bowl or food processor fitted with steel blades, beat together margarine, sweetener, and vanilla until creamy.

Add dry ingredients to creamed mixture and mix only until ingredients are blended. Transfer dough to pastry board and knead gently for a minute or two until mixture holds together.

Use fingers to spread dough into prepared pan. Bake until top is golden brown, about 25 to 30 minutes. Let cookies cool in pan on cake rack for 10 minutes. *Meanwhile make glaze:* Heat sweetener and margarine just until margarine is melted. Let cool slightly and spoon over cookies. Cut cookies into squares while still warm.

Store airtight. If possible, keep for a day or two before serving to let flavors mellow.

❖ *CINNAMON GRAHAM CRACKERS* ❖

MAKES ABOUT 2 DOZEN

2½ cups whole wheat pastry flour *or* 1¾ cups whole
    wheat flour and ¾ cup unbleached all-purpose flour
1½ teaspoons ground cinnamon
 ¼ teaspoon salt (optional)
 6 tablespoons liquid (unfiltered apple juice, water, soy
    milk, or grain coffee substitute)
 6 tablespoons corn oil
 6 tablespoons natural liquid sweetener
 1 teaspoon vanilla extract

Natural liquid sweetener, ground cinnamon, and/or
date sugar (optional)
Carob Glaze (page 128) (optional)

Combine flour, cinnamon, and salt if desired in food processor fitted with steel blade or in mixing bowl and blend well. Combine all remaining ingredients in separate small bowl. If using processor, pour half of liquid mixture evenly over dry ingredients and blend several seconds; add remaining liquid and blend several more seconds (do not overprocess or cookies will be tough). If mixing by hand, make well in center of dry ingredients. Pour in liquid mixture all at once and stir with fork briskly but gently until flour is evenly moistened. Form dough into ball and wrap in foil or plastic. Refrigerate 2 hours.

Preheat oven to 350°F. Roll dough out between sheets of waxed paper to thickness of ¼ inch. Cut dough into squares or bars using lightly floured pastry wheel or knife. Transfer to baking sheets. Prick lightly with fork. Bake until golden, about 15 to 17 minutes. Transfer to racks to cool. If desired, brush warm cookies with additional liquid sweetener and sprinkle with cinnamon and/or date sugar. For a special treat, cookies can be dipped in carob glaze.

Pies, Tarts, and Puff Pastry

Pies

EASY-AS-PIE FLAKY PASTRY

RICH FLAKY PIECRUST

EXTRA-FLAKY PIECRUST

WHOLE WHEAT PASTRY

GRAHAM CRACKER CRUST

CAROB–NUT CRUST

GINGER–SPICE CRUST

OAT–SPICE CRUST

TOASTED COCONUT–CAROB PIE SHELL

FAVORITE APPLE PIE

BLUEBERRY PIE

BLUEBERRY CREME PIE

GERMAN CHERRY PIE

SUMMER PEACH PIE

RASPBERRY–PEAR PIE

STRAWBERRY–RHUBARB PIE

BASIC CREME PIE

BANANA–NUT CREME PIE

BLUEBERRY MARBLE PIE

CAROB CHIP CREME PIE

NO-BAKE BANANA DREAM PIE

MELON–FIG PIE

PUMPKIN–PEACHES 'N' CREME PIE

SOUTHERN PECAN PIE

CHESTNUT–YAM PIE
SWEET POTATO PIE WITH TOFFEE CRUNCH TOPPING

Tarts
BASIC WHOLE WHEAT TART CRUST
FRESH FRUIT TARTS
AMBROSIA FRUIT TARTS
FRENCH APPLE–RAISIN TART
APPLE, PEAR, AND CHESTNUT TART
HAWAIIAN PINEAPPLE–COCONUT TART
LEMONY ORANGE CUSTARD TART
FRANGIPANE–PEAR TART
CAROB–TANGERINE TART
UPSIDE-DOWN FRESH FRUIT TART
CAROB–WALNUT TART
LINZERTORTE
FAVORITE FILLED TARTLETS

Puff pastry
WHOLE WHEAT PUFF PASTRY
PETITE PASTRY SHELLS
FLAN OR TART CASE (VOL-AU-VENT)
CORNUCOPIAS
FILLED CAKE
NAPOLEONS
POACHED FRUIT IN PASTRY
PETITE PALMIERS
PINWHEELS
TURNOVERS

PIES

Apple, pumpkin, chocolate cream, coconut custard, pecan, and lemon meringue are just a few of America's favorite pies. The pie as a dessert evolved in early American kitchens, inspired by its European cousin, the tart. Pies and tarts are frequently thought of as one and the same, but they really are not. A piecrust should be light and flaky but a tart crust is crisp, rich, and crumbly. The pie-filling list is extensive, whereas tarts are traditionally filled with fruits, pastry cream, or custard (though nowadays, creative license allows any combination of crust and filling for both pies and tarts). Pies are usually covered with a crust or lattice pastry strips; tarts, which are open-face, may be topped with a light fruit glaze or grated nuts.

Once you get the hang of it pies are among the easier desserts to prepare, yet the popularity of frozen or prepackaged piecrusts and canned fillings continues to grow. Mastering a flaky piecrust takes some practice, so be sure to follow the step-by-step instructions. A fine crust can be quickly made in the food processor, but it must be done with care or the dough will be tough. The processor is especially helpful in whipping up a fast filling.

Not even a scrumptious filling can save a soggy or tough piecrust. Here are some tips for a perfect crust:

1. Cutting the shortening into the dry ingredients is the first and most important step. If mixing by hand, the dry ingredients are measured into a large bowl. Vegetable oil—well chilled—is drizzled through the flour mixture and gently tossed with a fork. Vegetable or soy margarine should be chilled, cut into 1-inch pieces, and then blended into the flour with a pastry blender or with the fingers.

The food processor method is fast and easy. Insert the steel blade. Place the flour in the work bowl and blend in the oil or the margarine pieces using the pulse button or quick on/off turns.

Whether the shortening is cut in by hand or by machine, the mixture should resemble coarse breadcrumbs; the fat and flour should not be totally blended.

2. The liquid should be ice cold and sprinkled lightly over the fat/flour mixture. (A dash of vinegar added to the liquid will help to make a flakier crust.) Toss gently with a fork to moisten, adding a few drops more liquid if needed, and shape the dough into a ball; do not overwork the dough or it will be tough. Wrap the dough in plastic or waxed paper, flatten it into a disc, and chill for at least 1 hour. If using a food processor, sprinkle the liquid over the fat/flour mixture in the work bowl and blend only until the dough forms a ball and moves away from the sides of the bowl; do not overprocess.

The dough must be handled gently at all times so that the gluten in the flour does not develop. Whole-grain and soft-wheat pastry flours, which are lower in gluten content than regular all-purpose flour, make exceptionally flaky crusts.

3. Roll the dough out on a lightly floured work surface or floured pastry cloth (see note) into a circle 1½ inches larger in diameter than the pie pan. Use light strokes and roll out from the center of the dough toward the edges, checking frequently to see if the dough is sticking. If so, lift the dough gently, sprinkle a small amount of flour under the trouble spot, and continue rolling.

NOTE: *Pastry cloths or canvases can be purchased in specialty kitchenware stores. When floured, they keep the dough from sticking to the work surface.*

4. Transfer the rolled dough circle to the pie pan by draping the dough over the rolling pin. Ease the dough into the pan, pressing gently against the pan's sides; do not pull or stretch the dough, because this can cause cracks or shrinkage during baking. Trim the edges evenly.

5. Decorative edges are easy to do and can make all the difference in visual appeal. Some methods for decorating the pastry edge follow:

- Press floured fork tines into the pastry around the edge of pan.
- Flute the dough with your fingers.
- Roll out two strips of dough from scraps; twist them together into a coil or lap the strips over each other in a braid. Lightly brush the edge of the pastry in the pie pan with a mixture of 1 teaspoon arrowroot and enough water to form a paste. Place the coiled or braided strips on top.
- For a double-crust pie, lay the top crust over the filled pie and press the pastry edges together. Decorate using any of the methods just listed.

6. Chilling the pastry before baking makes a flakier crust.

7. When using a liquid pie filling it is best to bake the crust partially first. To prevent the crust from shrinking during baking, prick it all over with fork. Line it with waxed paper and weight it with an ovenproof plate, or else fill with dried beans, rice, or pie weights (see note, p. 60). Bake in a preheated 400°F oven until golden, about 9 minutes. Reduce heat to 375°F, remove plate or weights and waxed paper, and continue baking until the crust is either firm and barely golden (for a partially baked crust) or completely baked. Cool completely before filling to prevent cracking.

8. Before adding a cooked filling to a fully baked pie crust, lightly brush the crust with 1 teaspoon arrowroot or kuzu powder mixed with enough water to form a paste. Let the mixture dry, then add the filling. "Sealing" with the arrowroot mixture will help keep the crust from becoming soggy; brushing a small amount of margarine over the crust will achieve the same end.

❖ EASY-AS-PIE FLAKY PASTRY ❖

MAKES ONE 9-INCH CRUST

1½ cups whole wheat pastry flour
¼ teaspoon salt (optional)
¼ cup corn oil, chilled; or 5 tablespoons margarine, chilled
   and cut into 1-inch pieces
¼ cup ice water
¼ teaspoon apple cider vinegar

By hand: Combine flour and salt in large bowl. Drizzle oil over dry ingredients and toss gently with fork until mixture resembles coarse crumbs. Make well in center and pour in water and vinegar all at once, stirring briskly but lightly from center until dough holds together. Form into ball and wrap in waxed paper or plastic. Flatten dough into disc and chill at least 1 hour before rolling.

In food processor: Combine flour and salt in work bowl fitted with steel blade. Drizzle oil over dry ingredients and blend using pulse button or several on/off turns until mixture resembles coarse crumbs. Add water and vinegar and blend until dough pulls away from sides of work bowl. Remove dough from work bowl and form into ball. Wrap in waxed paper or plastic, flatten into disc, and chill at least 1 hour.

VARIATIONS:

Add 1 teaspoon ground cinnamon and ¼ teaspoon freshly grated nutmeg, or substitute chilled unfiltered apple juice, herb tea, grain coffee substitute, or decaffeinated coffee for water.

For two-crust or lattice-topped pie: Prepare as above using 2 cups whole wheat pastry flour, ½ teaspoon salt (optional), ⅔ cup minus 1 tablespoon corn oil or ⅔ cup chilled margarine, 7 to 8 tablespoons ice water, and ½ teaspoon apple cider vinegar.

NOTE: *Rice or beans can be cooled and stored for repeated use in weighing crusts. Pie weights, little metal pellets especially made for the job, are available in specialty kitchenware stores.*

·:· RICH FLAKY PIECRUST ·:·

This pastry can be used for either a pie or a tart crust; it is flaky, but has something of a cookielike texture as well.

MAKES TWO 8- OR 9-INCH CRUSTS

1 cup unbleached all-purpose flour and 1 cup whole wheat flour or 2 cups whole wheat pastry flour
1 tablespoon natural liquid sweetener
½ cup (1 stick) plus 3 tablespoons margarine, chilled and cut into 1-inch pieces
2 tablespoons corn oil, chilled
6 tablespoons ice water
¼ teaspoon apple cider vinegar

By hand: Place flour in large bowl. Drizzle in sweetener. Cut in margarine and oil with pastry blender until mixture resembles coarse crumbs. Sprinkle water and vinegar over mixture and toss lightly with fork until dough holds together. Form into ball and wrap in waxed paper or plastic. Flatten dough into disc and chill at least 1 hour before rolling.

In food processor: Place flour in work bowl fitted with steel blade. Drizzle in sweetener. Add margarine and oil and blend until mixture resembles coarse crumbs. Sprinkle in water and vinegar and blend until dough pulls away from the sides of work bowl. Remove dough from work bowl and form into ball. Wrap in waxed paper or plastic, flatten into disc, and chill at least 1 hour.

·:· EXTRA-FLAKY PIECRUST ·:·

MAKES TWO 9-INCH CRUSTS OR ONE 2-CRUST OR LATTICE TOPPED PIE

2½ cups whole wheat pastry flour
¼ cup corn oil, chilled
6 tablespoons margarine, chilled and cut into 1-inch pieces
7 tablespoons ice water
¼ teaspoon apple cider vinegar

2 tablespoons margarine, softened

By hand: Place flour in large bowl. Drizzle oil over flour. Cut in chilled margarine with pastry blender until mixture resembles coarse crumbs. Sprinkle water and vinegar over mixture and toss lightly with fork until dough holds together. Form into ball and wrap in waxed paper or plastic. Flatten dough into disc and chill at least 1 hour before rolling.

In food processor: Place flour in work bowl fitted with steel blade. Drizzle in oil. Add margarine and blend until mixture resembles coarse crumbs. Sprinkle in water and vinegar and blend until dough pulls away from sides of work bowl. Remove dough from work bowl and form into ball. Wrap in waxed paper or plastic, flatten into disc, and chill at least 1 hour.

Roll dough out into 4-inch circle. Spread with 1 tablespoon softened margarine. Fold dough in half and spread with remaining 1 tablespoon margarine. Fold in half again and roll out to desired size.

❖ WHOLE WHEAT PASTRY ❖

MAKES TWO 9-INCH CRUSTS

---

2 cups whole wheat flour
¼ cup wheat germ
¼ teaspoon salt (optional)
1 tablespoon natural liquid sweetener
1 cup (2 sticks) margarine, chilled and cut into 1-inch pieces
¼ cup ice water
¼ teaspoon apple cider vinegar

By hand: Combine flour, wheat germ, and salt in large bowl. Drizzle sweetener over dry ingredients. Cut in margarine with pastry blender until mixture resembles coarse crumbs. Sprinkle water and vinegar over mixture and toss lightly with fork until dough holds together. Form into ball and wrap in waxed paper or plastic. Flatten dough into disc and chill at least 1 hour before rolling.

In food processor: Combine flour, wheat germ, and salt in work bowl fitted with steel blade. Drizzle sweetener over dry ingredients. Add margarine and blend until mixture resembles coarse crumbs. Sprinkle in water and vinegar and blend just until dough pulls away from sides of work bowl. Remove dough from work bowl and form into ball. Wrap in waxed paper or plastic, flatten into disc, and chill at least 1 hour.

VARIATIONS:

Add spices or substitute liquid as in Easy-as-Pie Flaky Pastry (page 60); substitute other whole-grain flour(s) for up to ¾ cup whole wheat flour.

❖ *GRAHAM CRACKER CRUST* ❖

MAKES ONE 9- OR 10-INCH CRUST

---

2 cups finely crushed graham cracker crumbs
1 teaspoon ground cinnamon (optional)
½ cup (1 stick) margarine, melted
2 tablespoons natural liquid sweetener
1 to 2 tablespoons liquid (water, unfiltered apple juice, or
    grain coffee substitute)

Combine crumbs and cinnamon in medium bowl. Drizzle with margarine and sweetener and toss until evenly moistened, adding water or other liquid if necessary to make crumbs hold together. Press mixture evenly into pie pan. Chill thoroughly before filling.

VARIATIONS:

Substitute ½ cup finely chopped nuts for ½ cup crumbs.

Use any favorite cookie, cracker, or cereal, crushed to fine crumbs, in place of graham crackers.

❖ *CAROB–NUT CRUST* ❖

This crust is protein-packed and very rich. For those allergic to wheat products the mixture can be cut into small pieces for a delicious confection. Use with a cooked filling, since this crust requires no baking.

MAKES ONE 10-INCH CRUST

---

  2 cups ground nuts (cashews, pecans, almonds, walnuts, or peanuts), lightly toasted

¾ cup sesame seeds, lightly toasted

½ cup unsweetened carob powder, lightly toasted (see note)

  1 teaspoon ground cinnamon

  3 tablespoons natural liquid sweetener

  2 tablespoons corn oil, chilled

Lightly oil 10-inch pie pan or coat with slightly warmed liquid lecithin. Combine nuts, sesame seeds, carob, and cinnamon in large bowl. Blend sweetener and oil and add to nut mixture. Knead in bowl until mixture holds together. Press firmly and evenly into prepared pan. Chill at least 1 hour before filling.

Suggested fillings: Carob–Mint Pie Filling (page 75), or "creme" pie filling of your choice.

NOTE: *To toast carob powder, spread on cookie sheet or in shallow baking pan and place in 250°F oven until it turns slightly darker. This should take only a few minutes. Watch carefully to make sure it doesn't burn.*

❖ GINGER–SPICE CRUST ❖

This pastry is like a cookie dough—if there's any extra, get out the cookie cutters.

MAKES ONE 9-INCH CRUST

1½ cups whole wheat pastry flour
1½ teaspoons ground ginger
  1 teaspoon ground cinnamon
  ½ teaspoon ground allspice
  ¼ cup natural liquid sweetener
  1 heaping tablespoon blackstrap molasses
  ½ cup corn oil or margarine, chilled
3 to 4 tablespoons liquid (ice water, chilled grain coffee
    substitute, or chilled decaffeinated coffee)

Combine dry ingredients in large bowl. Drizzle in sweetener and molasses and toss with fork. Cut in oil or margarine with pastry blender until mixture resembles coarse crumbs. Sprinkle liquid over mixture and toss lightly with fork until dough holds together, adding a few drops more water if necessary. Form into ball and wrap in waxed paper or plastic. Flatten dough into disc and chill at least 1 hour before rolling.

❖ OAT–SPICE CRUST ❖

MAKES ONE 9-INCH CRUST

  ¼ cup margarine or corn oil
  ¼ cup natural liquid sweetener
  ¼ cup unfiltered apple juice
  2 cups rolled oats
  ¼ cup whole-grain flour
1½ teaspoons ground cinnamon

Combine margarine, sweetener, and apple juice in medium-size saucepan or skillet and simmer, stirring, over medium heat until margarine is melted, about 3 minutes. Stir in oats, flour, and cinnamon all at once, reduce heat to low, and cook until mixture begins to pull away from sides of pan. Let cool.

Lightly oil 9-inch pie pan, or coat with liquid lecithin. Pat crust mixture into pan to thickness of ¼ inch. Fill and bake.

❖ *TOASTED COCONUT–CAROB PIE SHELL* ❖

Although not always available, freshly grated coconut is a treat. I grate the meat of a whole coconut, toast it lightly in the oven, and use it in this crust, in No-Bake Coconut Macaroons (page 34), or sprinkled on cereal. Unsweetened grated coconut can also be purchased in natural foods stores.

MAKES ONE 9-INCH CRUST

---

2 cups freshly grated coconut
¼ cup (½ stick) margarine, melted and cooled
2 tablespoons unsweetened carob powder
2 tablespoons natural liquid sweetener
½ teaspoon vanilla extract

Preheat oven to 400°F. Lightly grease rimmed baking sheet. Spread coconut evenly on sheet. Bake, stirring once or twice, until lightly and evenly browned, about 5 to 8 minutes. Let cool. Transfer to medium-size bowl.

Reduce oven temperature to 375°F. Combine all remaining ingredients in small saucepan and place over low heat until bubbly, stirring frequently. Pour over coconut and toss to moisten evenly. Press mixture into pie pan. Bake until lightly browned, about 8 minutes. Cool completely before filling. (Can be refrigerated at least 45 minutes instead of baked before filling, but baking will make a more cohesive crust.)

⦂⦂ FAVORITE APPLE PIE ⦂⦂

The inspiration for this book came the summer I spent developing dessert recipes for the Yarrowstalk, a macrobiotic restaurant in Boulder, Colorado. This was one of the most popular pies at the restaurant—the slices were so big that we always served them with at least two forks! For special occasions, serve pie warm topped with Real Vanilla Bean Ice Creme (page 210).

MAKES ONE 9- TO 10-INCH PIE

---

6 to 7 large cooking apples, peeled, cored, and thinly sliced
½ cup natural liquid sweetener
½ cup Rice Creme (page 171), mixed with 1 tablespoon fresh lemon juice, or ½ cup Soy Sour Cream (page 172)
½ cup raisins
¼ cup chopped pecans or walnuts (optional)
3 tablespoons whole wheat pastry flour or 1½ tablespoons arrowroot
1½ teaspoons vanilla extract
1 teaspoon ground cinnamon
½ teaspoon freshly grated nutmeg
Oat–Spice Crust (page 65)
1 tablespoon margarine
Streusel topping (page 174)

Preheat oven to 425°F. Combine apples, sweetener, rice cream or soy sour cream, raisins, nuts, flour or arrowroot, vanilla, and spices in large bowl and toss to blend well. Pour into crust, heaping filling higher in center. Dot with margarine. Sprinkle evenly with topping (pie will be very full). Set on baking sheet to catch any overflowing juices. Bake 15 minutes. Reduce heat to 350°F and bake until filling is bubbly, about 30 minutes. Serve warm or at room temperature.

❖ *BLUEBERRY PIE* ❖

MAKES ONE 9-INCH PIE

---

4 cups blueberries, sorted, rinsed, and drained
½ cup natural liquid sweetener
3 tablespoons unbleached all-purpose flour or 2
  tablespoons arrowroot or 1¼ tablespoons kuzu powder
½ teaspoon vanilla extract
½ teaspoon grated lemon peel
½ teaspoon ground cinnamon
  Unbaked piecrust
  Lattice pastry strips

Preheat oven to 400°F. Combine blueberries, sweetener, flour or arrowroot or kuzu, vanilla, lemon peel, and cinnamon in large bowl and toss lightly with wooden or stainless-steel spoon. Pour into crust. Top with lattice strips or cinnamon topping. Bake 10 minutes. Reduce heat to 350°F and bake until filling is bubbly, about 25 to 30 minutes. Serve warm or at room temperature.

VARIATIONS:

Substitute strawberries, raspberries, or blackberries for 1 cup of the blueberries.

❖ *BLUEBERRY CREME PIE* ❖

MAKES ONE 10-INCH PIE

---

4 cups blueberries, sorted, rinsed, and drained
½ cup natural liquid sweetener
2½ tablespoons arrowroot
½ teaspoon vanilla extract
½ cup Rice Creme (page 171)
¼ cup finely ground blanched almonds
  Unbaked piecrust with lattice pastry topping
  Natural liquid sweetener and finely chopped toasted
  almonds (optional)

Preheat oven to 400°F. Combine blueberries, ½ cup sweetener, arrow-root, and vanilla in large bowl and toss lightly with wooden or stainless-steel spoon. Blend rice creme with ground almonds in small bowl. Add to blueberry mixture and toss well. Pour into crust. Top with lattice strips. Bake 10 minutes. Reduce heat to 350°F and bake until filling is bubbly, about 25 to 30 minutes. If desired, brush warm pie lightly with liquid sweetener and sprinkle with chopped almonds. Serve warm or at room temperature.

❖ GERMAN CHERRY PIE ❖

MAKES ONE 8-INCH PIE

---

3 cups cherries, pitted
½ to ¾ cup natural liquid sweetener (depending on
    sweetness of cherries)
3 tablespoons unbleached all-purpose flour or 2
    tablespoons arrowroot
1 teaspoon grated lemon or orange peel
    Unbaked crust for two-crust pie (spiced Whole
    Wheat Pastry, page 62, is particularly good)
    Creamy Soy Whip (page 173) and chopped toasted
    almonds (optional garnishes)

Preheat oven to 400°F. Combine cherries, sweetener, flour, and lemon peel in large bowl and toss to blend well. Pour into crust. Top with lattice pastry strips or top crust; if using top crust, cut several slashes for steam to escape. Bake 10 minutes. Reduce heat to 350°F and bake until filling is bubbly, about 25 minutes. Serve warm or at room temperature. Garnish with soy whip and chopped almonds if desired.

❖ *SUMMER PEACH PIE* ❖

MAKES ONE 9-INCH PIE

---

　1 tablespoon whole wheat pastry flour
½ teaspoon ground cinnamon
½ teaspoon ground ginger
¼ teaspoon ground allspice
　6 large ripe peaches, pitted and cut into ¼-inch-thick slices
½ cup natural liquid sweetener
　　Unbaked crust for two-crust pie
　1 tablespoon margarine

Preheat oven to 425°F. Combine flour and spices in cup. Place peaches in large bowl, add flour mixture, and toss to coat. Drizzle in sweetener and toss gently. Pour into crust. Dot with margarine. Cover with top crust; cut several slashes for steam to escape. Bake 15 minutes. Reduce heat to 375°F and bake until filling is bubbly, about 35 to 40 minutes. Serve warm or at room temperature.

VARIATIONS:

Substitute apricots, apples, or plums for peaches.

❖ *RASPBERRY–PEAR PIE* ❖

MAKES ONE 9-INCH PIE

---

　1 cup fresh or frozen unsweetened raspberries
½ cup natural liquid sweetener
　1 tablespoon arrowroot or 1 teaspoon kuzu powder
　1 teaspoon fresh lemon juice

　8 medium-size ripe pears
　　Unbaked crust for two-crust pie
　1 tablespoon margarine
　　Natural liquid sweetener (optional)

Preheat oven to 400°F. Combine raspberries, sweetener, arrowroot or kuzu and lemon juice in food processor or blender and puree several seconds; do not completely liquefy berries. Refrigerate while preparing pears.

Core pears; cut into ¼-inch-thick slices. If pears are very juicy, toss slices with up to 1 teaspoon additional arrowroot. Arrange in circular decorative pattern in crust. Pour raspberry mixture over. Dot with margarine. Top with lattice pastry strips. Bake 10 minutes. Reduce heat to 350°F and bake until filling is bubbly, about 30 to 35 minutes, brushing lattice with additional sweetener during last few minutes of baking to glaze if desired. Serve warm or at room temperature.

❖ *STRAWBERRY–RHUBARB PIE* ❖

MAKES ONE 9-INCH PIE

½ cup natural liquid sweetener
3 tablespoons arrowroot or 1½ tablespoons kuzu powder
¼ teaspoon ground cinnamon
¼ teaspoon allspice
2¾ cups rhubarb, cut into ½-inch pieces
1 cup sliced strawberries
Unbaked crust for two-crust pie
1 tablespoon margarine

Preheat oven to 400°F. Combine sweetener, arrowroot, and spices in large bowl and blend well. Add fruit and toss gently to coat. Pour into crust. Dot with margarine. Top with lattice pastry strips. Bake 10 minutes. Reduce heat to 350°F and bake until filling is bubbly, about 35 to 40 minutes. Serve warm or at room temperature.

VARIATIONS:

Substitute raspberries or chopped apple for either fruit.

∴ BASIC CREME PIE ∴

Tofu gives this pie filling a texture resembling cheesecake. Though tofu is often thought of as "beyond bland," this is actually an asset when you are adding your own flavorings.

MAKES ONE 9-INCH PIE

BASIC TOFU CREME FILLING:

3½ cups tofu

1 cup liquid (fruit juice, grain coffee substitute, decaffeinated coffee, herb tea, nut milk, soy milk, or water)

½ cup natural liquid sweetener (a few more tablespoons can be added, if desired, without affecting filling texture)

½ cup corn oil or margarine, melted

1½ teaspoons vanilla extract

Graham Cracker (or cookie crumb) Crust (page 63), well chilled

Combine tofu, liquid, sweetener, oil or margarine and vanilla in food processor fitted with steel blade and puree until smooth. Pour into crust. Chill at least 2 hours before serving.

VARIATIONS:

Add ½ cup unsweetened carob chips or ¼ cup lightly toasted unsweetened carob powder (see page 64).

Add 3 to 4 tablespoons nut butter.

Chestnut Creme Filling: Add 1 cup sliced chestnuts (see page 80 for peeling directions).

Add 1 teaspoon grated lemon or orange peel, substituting the citrus juice for part of required liquid.

Soak ¼ cup chopped dried fruit overnight in required liquid. Drain; use liquid in recipe and stir fruit into pureed mixture.

Prepare half of filling recipe; spread in crust and chill. Shortly before serving, top decoratively with fresh or cooked fruit. Brush with Apple Glaze (page 122) or Maple Glaze (page 179) or garnish with rosettes of Creamy Soy Whip (page 173) if desired.

For marble swirl pie, remove ½ cup of filling mixture. Blend in enough unsweetened carob powder, fresh mint juice (see note), or beet or cherry juice to tint filling to desired color. Alternate dollops of plain and tinted filling in crust, then swirl through with knife to marbleize.

NOTE: *To get fresh mint juice soak several sprigs of mint leaves in ½ cup of water overnight. Discard mint leaves before using. Or, use ¼ teaspoon alcohol-free mint flavoring, available in health food stores.*

❖ *BANANA–NUT CREME PIE* ❖

MAKES ONE 9-INCH DEEP-DISH PIE

FILLING:
- ½ cup soy milk or nut milk
- 1½ tablespoons agar-agar flakes

- 2 cups tofu
- 2 medium-size ripe bananas
- ½ cup natural liquid sweetener
- 5 tablespoons corn oil or margarine, melted
- 2 teaspoons fresh lemon juice
- 1 teaspoon vanilla extract
- 1 teaspoon ground cinnamon
- ½ cup chopped toasted nuts
  Graham Cracker (or cookie crumb) Crust (page 63), well chilled, or baked pie shell

TOPPING:
- 1 medium-size ripe banana, sliced
- 1 teaspoon natural liquid sweetener
- ½ teaspoon fresh lemon juice
  Cookie crumbs or Creamy Soy Whip (page 173)
  (optional garnishes)

For filling: Place soy milk in small saucepan. Add agar-agar and bring to boil over medium-high heat. Reduce heat and simmer until agar-agar is completely dissolved, about 2 to 3 minutes. Let cool slightly.

Combine tofu, bananas, sweetener, oil or margarine, lemon juice, vanilla, and cinnamon in food processor and blend until smooth. Add agar-agar mixture and blend until thick and creamy. Stir in chopped nuts. Pour into crust. Chill at least 3 hours. *(recipe continues)*

For topping: Just before serving, combine remaining banana, sweetener, and lemon juice in small bowl and toss gently. Arrange decoratively over filling. Garnish with cookie crumbs or soy whip rosettes if desired.

∙:∙ *BLUEBERRY MARBLE PIE* ∙:∙

Almost a cheesecake! And the tofu provides a nutrition boost.

MAKES ONE 9- OR 10-INCH PIE

---

2 cups blueberries, sorted, rinsed, and drained
¾ cup natural liquid sweetener
1½ tablespoons unbleached all-purpose flour or 1 tablespoon arrowroot or 1½ generous teaspoons kuzu powder
1¾ teaspoons vanilla extract
¼ teaspoon grated lemon peel
¼ teaspoon ground cinnamon
2½ cups tofu, squeezed in towel to remove excess water
¼ cup Frangipane Filling (page 90) or cashew butter (page 170)
1 tablespoon fresh lemon juice
2 tablespoons water or soy milk
1½ tablespoons arrowroot or 2 teaspoons kuzu powder
Oat–Spice Crust (page 65)
¾ cup Creamy Tofu Cheese Filling (page 175)

Preheat oven to 350°F. Combine blueberries, ¼ cup sweetener, flour, ¼ teaspoon vanilla, lemon peel, and cinnamon in medium-size bowl and toss lightly with wooden or stainless-steel spoon. Set aside.

Place tofu in large bowl or in food processor fitted with steel blade and blend well. Add remaining ½ cup sweetener, almond paste or cashew butter, lemon juice, and remaining 1½ teaspoons vanilla. Blend water or soy milk and arrowroot or kuzu in cup, add to tofu mixture, and blend well. Pour into crust. Top with blueberry mixture and swirl through several times with knife to marbleize. Bake until tester inserted in center comes out clean, about 35 minutes. Let cool, then chill. Pipe rosettes around inside of crust with tofu cheese filling and serve.

VARIATIONS:

Substitute other fresh or frozen unsweetened berries for blueberries.

Bake in tartlet pans lined with partially baked crust.

Substitute ½ teaspoon almond extract for vanilla in tofu mixture.

Color tofu mixture with cherry or beet juice.

∙∴∙ CAROB CHIP CREME PIE ∙∴∙

MAKES ONE 9-INCH PIE

---

  1 cup liquid (grain coffee substitute, decaffeinated coffee,
     or soy milk)
1½ tablespoons agar-agar flakes

2¾ cups tofu
  ½ cup natural liquid sweetener
  ½ cup corn oil or margarine, melted
  3 tablespoons unsweetened carob powder, lightly toasted
     (see note, p. 64)
  1 teaspoon vanilla extract
  ½ cup unsweetened carob chips
     Carob–Nut Crust (page 64), well chilled
     Finely chopped nuts or crushed cookie crumbs (optional
     garnishes)

Place coffee or soy milk in small saucepan. Add agar-agar and bring to boil over medium-high heat. Reduce heat and simmer until agar-agar is completely dissolved, about 2 to 3 minutes. Let cool slightly.

Combine tofu, sweetener, ¼ cup oil, carob powder, and vanilla in processor or blender and mix until smooth. Add agar-agar mixture and remaining ¼ cup oil and blend until thick and creamy. Stir in carob chips. Pour into crust. Sprinkle with nuts or crumbs if desired. Chill at least 2 hours before serving.

VARIATIONS:

Carob-Mint Pie Filling: For "grasshopper pie," soak several sprigs fresh mint overnight in the coffee or soy milk. Discard mint before adding agar-agar.

For a completely dairy-free pie, substitute ¼ cup coarsely broken carob cookies for carob chips.

❖ *NO–BAKE BANANA DREAM PIE* ❖

MAKES ONE 9- OR 10-INCH PIE

FILLING:
½ cup water
2½ tablespoons agar-agar flakes

2½ cups Rice Creme or Oat Creme (page 171)
2 ripe (but not overripe) bananas
1 teaspoon fresh lemon juice
1 teaspoon ground cinnamon
⅛ teaspoon freshly grated nutmeg
Carob–Nut Crust (page 64), well chilled

TOPPING:
1 large or 2 small ripe bananas
½ teaspoon fresh lemon juice
Finely crushed graham cracker or gingersnap crumbs (optional)
Lemon- or carob-flavored Soy Whip or Soy Sour Cream (pages 172–73) (optional)

For filling: Place water in small saucepan. Add agar-agar and bring to boil over medium-high heat. Reduce heat and simmer until agar-agar is completely dissolved, about 2 to 3 minutes. Let cool slightly.

Combine rice or oat creme, bananas, lemon juice, and spices in food processor fitted with steel blade or blender and blend well but do not puree completely. Transfer to medium-size bowl. Add agar-agar mixture and stir to blend. Pour into crust. Chill thoroughly.

For topping: No more than 1 hour before serving, slice banana into small glass or stainless-steel bowl. Add lemon juice and toss gently to coat. Arrange decoratively over filling. Sprinkle crumbs evenly around crust edge. Decorate with rosettes of Soy Whip or Soy Sour Cream if desired.

❖ MELON–FIG PIE ❖

An unusual no-bake pie, refreshing on a warm summer evening.

MAKES ONE 10-INCH PIE

FILLING:

4½ cups ripe melon, peeled, seeded, and cut into small cubes (any sweet melon will do; I like a combination of honeydew, cantaloupe, and casaba)

¼ cup natural liquid sweetener

1 teaspoon fresh orange, lemon, or lime juice

½ cup water or unsweetened fruit juice

¼ cup agar-agar flakes

TOPPING:

½ cup mixed citrus or other fruit juices (if using citrus, use a combination or all orange; all lemon or lime juice will make topping too tart)

1 tablespoon arrowroot or 1 teaspoon kuzu powder

1 cup tofu

¼ cup finely chopped unsulfured dried figs

2 tablespoons natural liquid sweetener

Carob–Nut Crust (page 64), well chilled
Finely chopped pistachios, thinly sliced kiwi, or mint sprigs (garnish)

For filling: Combine melon, sweetener, and citrus juice in food processor fitted with steel blade or in blender and blend just until melon is coarsely pureed. Transfer to glass or stainless-steel bowl.

Place water or fruit juice in small saucepan. Add agar-agar and bring to boil over medium-high heat. Reduce heat and simmer until agar-agar is completely dissolved, about 2 to 3 minutes. Let cool. Add to melon mixture and stir gently to blend.

For topping: Combine mixed citrus or fruit juices with arrowroot or kuzu in small saucepan and simmer just until clear. Let cool slightly. Place in food processor or blender along with tofu, figs, and sweetener and blend until smooth.

Turn melon mixture into chilled crust. Spread with fig topping (topping can be piped through pastry bag if desired). Garnish with pistachios, kiwi, or mint. Chill until ready to serve.   *(recipe continues)*

VARIATION:

Substitute dates for figs. Decrease sweetener if desired.

❖ *PUMPKIN–PEACHES 'N' CREME PIE* ❖

This is a light chiffon-type pie that requires no baking. It is a delightful finale for an Indian-summer brunch.

MAKES ONE 9-INCH DEEP-DISH PIE

---

  1 cup unsweetened fruit juice or water
  2 tablespoons agar-agar flakes
  1 cup chopped peeled fresh or unsweetened frozen
    peaches
1½ cups pureed fresh-cooked or canned pumpkin
  ½ cup natural liquid sweetener
  2 teaspoons pumpkin pie spice *or* 1 teaspoon ground
    cinnamon, ½ teaspoon ground ginger, and ¼ teaspoon
    allspice.
    Gingersnap or Graham Cracker Crust (page 63), well
    chilled
    Apricot- or ginger-flavored Creamy Soy Whip (page
    173) (optional garnish)

Combine fruit juice and agar-agar in medium-size saucepan and bring to boil over medium-high heat. Reduce heat and simmer 3 minutes. Remove from heat and stir in peaches. Let stand 5 minutes. Blend in pumpkin, sweetener, and spice. Pour into crust. Chill at least 2 hours. Serve with flavored soy whip if desired.

❖ SOUTHERN PECAN PIE ❖

This pie may be smaller than usual, but it is also richer than usual; little slices will suffice.

MAKES ONE 8-INCH PIE

⅔ cup natural liquid sweetener
3 tablespoons margarine, melted and cooled
2 tablespoons blackstrap molasses
1 tablespoon liquid lecithin
1 teaspoon vanilla extract
1 cup grain coffee substitute or decaffeinated coffee
1 tablespoon arrowroot or 1 teaspoon kuzu powder
1 teaspoon ground cinnamon
⅛ teaspoon freshly grated nutmeg
1 cup halved or coarsely chopped pecans
Partially baked crust for one-crust pie
Spiced Creamy Soy Whip (page 173) and chopped pecans
(optional garnish)

Preheat oven to 350°F. Combine sweetener, margarine, molasses, lecithin, and vanilla in food processor or electric-mixer bowl and blend until smooth and thickened. In a small bowl combine coffee and arrowroot. Add to molasses mixture along with spices and blend well. Place pecans in crust. Turn filling into crust, spreading evenly. Bake until bubbly and browned, about 40 to 50 minutes, reducing heat to 325°F if crust browns too quickly. Serve warm or at room temperature. Garnish with soy whip and chopped pecans if desired.

VARIATIONS:

Substitute walnuts for pecans.

Add ¼ cup chopped dried apricots that have been soaked 2 hours in grain coffee substitute or decaffeinated coffee and drained well. Serve with apricot- or peach-flavored Creamy Soy Whip (page 173) or Real Vanilla Bean Ice Creme (page 210).

❖ *CHESTNUT–YAM PIE* ❖

*If the sweetener is omitted, this can be served as a vegetable course—
with or without crust.*

MAKES ONE 9-INCH PIE

---

   7 medium-size yams
1½ cups sliced peeled chestnuts (see note)
  ½ cup natural liquid sweetener
   3 tablespoons corn oil or margarine, melted
   1 teaspoon vanilla extract
   1 teaspoon ground cinnamon
  ½ teaspoon allspice
  ½ teaspoon ground ginger
1½ cups unfiltered apple juice
   2 tablespoons arrowroot or 1 tablespoon kuzu powder
  ½ cup soaked, drained, and chopped unsulfured dried
      fruit (optional)
   3 tablespoons finely chopped pecans (optional)
      Unbaked pie crust
   2 tablespoons vegetable or soy margarine
   2 tablespoons date sugar, mixed with ½ teaspoon ground
      cinnamon

Place yams in large saucepan, cover with water, and bring to boil. Boil
until yams are tender but not mushy, about 20 minutes, or longer, depending on their size. Drain and let cool.

Preheat oven to 350°F. Peel yams; cut into ¼-inch slices. Place in large
bowl. Add chestnuts, sweetener, oil vanilla, or kuzu and spices and toss
to blend. Combine apple juice and arrowroot or kuzu and stir into yam
mixture, adding fruit and/or pecans if desired. Pour into crust. Dot with
margarine. Bake until filling is set, about 35 to 40 minutes, sprinkling
with date sugar/cinnamon mixture 10 minutes before end of baking
time. Serve warm or at room temperature.

NOTE: *To peel chestnuts, pierce each with sharp knife. Place in large saucepan, cover with water, and bring to boil over high heat. Reduce heat and
simmer 30 minutes. Drain chestnuts; let stand until cool enough to handle. Peel and slice.*

❖ SWEET POTATO PIE WITH TOFFEE ❖ CRUNCH TOPPING

MAKES ONE 9-INCH PIE

FILLING:

2 cups cooked, peeled, and quartered sweet potatoes
1½ cups plus 2 tablespoons soy milk
⅔ cup natural liquid sweetener
3 teaspoons arrowroot or 2 teaspoons kuzu powder
2 teaspoons ground cinnamon
½ teaspoon ground allspice

TOPPING:

1½ cups whole wheat or whole wheat pastry flour
5 tablespoons margarine, melted, or corn oil
3 tablespoons natural liquid sweetener
3 tablespoons finely chopped nuts
1 teaspoon ground cinnamon
½ teaspoon ground ginger
2 to 3 tablespoons liquid (grain coffee substitute, decaffeinated coffee, or unsweetened fruit juice)
2 tablespoons vegetable or soy margarine (optional)

Ginger–Spice Crust (page 65), unbaked and well chilled

For filling: Preheat oven to 350°F. Puree or mash sweet potatoes in food processor fitted with steel blade or in large mixing bowl. Blend in soy milk, sweetener, arrowroot or kuzu, and spices. Set filling aside.

For topping: Combine flour, melted margarine or oil, sweetener, nuts, and spices in medium-size bowl and blend well. Sprinkle in liquid, adding only enough to make mixture crumbly; do not overmoisten.

Pour filling into crust. Sprinkle evenly with topping. Dot with margarine if desired. Bake until topping is crisp and golden, about 50 to 60 minutes. Serve warm or at room temperature.

TARTS

A delicate, melt-in-the-mouth tart is the perfect dessert. Tarts can be made in many shapes and sizes, using anything from a very large pan to tiny individual barquettes, tartlet tins, or even muffin pans. Though a tart crust is traditionally more cookielike in texture than a flaky pie crust, feel free to experiment by interchanging them. The same applies to fillings; nearly any pie filling will work in a tart as well, so be creative with your favorites.

❖ *BASIC WHOLE WHEAT TART CRUST* ❖

MAKES ONE 9-INCH OR TWO 4½-INCH TART SHELLS

---

      2 cups whole wheat pastry flour
      ½ teaspoon arrowroot
      ¼ teaspoon salt (optional)
    1½ tablespoons natural liquid sweetener (optional)
      1 teaspoon vanilla extract
      ½ teaspoon grated lemon peel
    10 tablespoons (1¼ sticks) margarine, chilled and cut
         into 1-inch pieces; or ½ cup (1 stick) margarine plus
         2 tablespoons corn oil, all chilled
3 to 4 tablespoons ice water

By hand: Combine flour, arrowroot, and salt in large bowl. Drizzle sweetener and vanilla over dry ingredients; sprinkle in lemon peel. Cut in shortening with pastry blender until mixture resembles coarse crumbs. Sprinkle water over mixture 1 tablespoonful at a time and toss lightly with fork until dough holds together. Form into ball and wrap in waxed paper or plastic. Flatten dough into disc and chill at least 1 hour before rolling.

In food processor: Combine flour, arrowroot, and salt in work bowl fitted with steel blade. Drizzle sweetener and vanilla over dry ingredients; sprinkle in lemon peel. Add shortening and blend until mixture resembles coarse crumbs. Sprinkle in water 1 tablespoonful at a time and blend just until dough pulls away from sides of work bowl. Remove dough from work bowl and form into ball. Wrap in waxed paper or plastic, flatten into disc, and chill at least 1 hour.

VARIATION:

Substitute ½ cup finely ground nuts for ½ cup flour.

❖ FRESH FRUIT TARTS ❖

Pastry creme can be topped with uncooked fruit, too; in this case, add fruit no more than 15 minutes before serving. For a variation, try substituting a layer of nut butter for pastry creme.

MAKES ONE 9-INCH TART OR TWO 4½-INCH TARTLETS

PASTRY CREME:
1 tablespoon arrowroot
1 cup soy milk
¼ cup natural liquid sweetener
1 teaspoon vanilla extract
1 teaspoon fresh lemon, orange, or other fruit juice (optional)

COOKED BERRY OR CHERRY TOPPING:
4 cups fresh blueberries, raspberries, blackberries, or pitted cherries *or* 12 ounces unsweetened frozen berries
¼ cup natural liquid sweetener
1 teaspoon fresh lemon juice
¼ teaspoon ground cinnamon or allspice
¼ cup water
1 teaspoon arrowroot

Basic Whole Wheat Tart Crust (page 83), baked

For pastry creme: Combine arrowroot with enough soy milk to form paste; set aside. Mix sweetener, vanilla, and remaining soy milk in medium-size saucepan and cook over medium heat until mixture begins to bubble. Whisk in arrowroot paste and continue cooking briefly until mixture coats back of spoon. Remove from heat and stir in fruit juice. Cover with waxed paper, placing paper directly on surface of pastry creme to prevent skin from forming. Chill thoroughly.

For fruit topping: Combine 2 cups berries, sweetener, lemon juice, and spice in large saucepan and bring to boil. Meanwhile, mix water and arrowroot to form paste. Stir into fruit mixture and simmer until thickened. Let cool to lukewarm, then stir in remaining berries.

Spread pastry creme in bottom of cooled tart shell(s). Top with cooked berry mixture, cover lightly with waxed paper, and chill. Remove from refrigerator 15 minutes before serving.

❖ *AMBROSIA FRUIT TARTS* ❖

Choose fresh peaches, pears, apples, apricots, nectarines, plums, or oranges in creative combinations that are pleasing to both eye and palate. Other brightly colored fruits, such as strawberries, sliced kiwi, or seeded grapes, can be added as garnish.

MAKES ONE 9- TO 10-INCH TART OR TWO 4½-INCH TARTLETS

1¼ cups water
¼ cup natural liquid sweetener
1 2-inch strip lemon peel
1 teaspoon vanilla extract
5 medium-size fruits (from above list), peeled if necessary, pitted, and cut into ¼-inch-thick slices

Pastry Creme (page 84), Rice Creme (page 171), or nut butter (page 170)
Basic Whole Wheat Tart Crust (p. 83), baked

Combine water, sweetener, lemon peel, and vanilla in large saucepan and bring to boil over medium-high heat. Reduce heat to medium-low and simmer 3 minutes. Add fruit, cover, and poach until tender, about 10 to 12 minutes. Remove fruit with slotted spoon. *To make the Fruit Glaze:* Increase heat to high and boil syrup until reduced to glaze consistency.

Spread pastry, rice creme, or nut butter in bottom of cooled tart shell(s). Arrange poached fruit decoratively over filling. Brush with glaze. Chill until serving time.

VARIATION:

Substitute carob frosting (page 172) for pastry creme; top with sliced bananas that have been tossed with 1 tablespoon each liquid sweetener and fresh lemon juice. Add sliced strawberries if desired.

❖ FRENCH APPLE–RAISIN TART ❖

MAKES ONE 9-INCH TART

---

5 large tart baking apples, peeled and cored
Fresh lemon juice

¼ cup natural liquid sweetener
3 tablespoons margarine
2 tablespoons liquid (unfiltered apple juice, grain coffee substitute, or decaffeinated coffee)
1½ teaspoons ground cinnamon
1 teaspoon vanilla extract
¼ teaspoon freshly grated nutmeg
¾ cup (4 ounces) raisins or dried currants

Basic Whole Wheat Tart Crust (page 83), unbaked and to which 1 teaspoon ground cinnamon and ½ teaspoon ground allspice have been added to dry ingredients before cutting in margarine
Date sugar, cookie crumbs, or finely chopped nuts (optional garnishes)

Slice apples ¼ inch thick. Place in large bowl and toss with lemon juice to prevent discoloration.

Combine sweetener, margarine, liquid, cinnamon, vanilla, and nutmeg in large saucepan and place over medium heat until margarine is melted, stirring occasionally. Add apple slices and simmer until crisp-tender, about 6 to 8 minutes, turning gently with wooden spoon. Remove from heat and stir in raisins. Let mixture cool.

Position rack in lower third of oven and preheat to 400°F. Partially bake shell for 8-10 minutes, or until it turns a light golden color; retain oven temperature. Let pastry cool. Arrange apple slices decoratively in shell, starting at outer edge. Bake 10 minutes. Reduce oven temperature to 350°F and bake until apples are tender, about 25 to 30 minutes. Garnish as desired. Serve tart warm or at room temperature.

❖ APPLE, PEAR, AND CHESTNUT TART ❖

MAKES ONE 9-INCH TART

2 large baking apples, peeled, cored, and cut into ¼-inch-thick slices
1 teaspoon fresh lemon juice
2 ripe pears

Chestnut Creme Filling (page 72)
Basic Whole Wheat Tart Crust (page 83), partially baked
2 tablespoons natural liquid sweetener or date sugar
1½ tablespoons margarine, melted
1 teaspoon ground cinnamon

Sprinkle apple slices with ½ teaspoon lemon juice and toss lightly; set aside. Bring large saucepan of water to boil over high heat. Add pears and blanch 2 minutes, then plunge into cold water to stop cooking process. When cool enough to handle, peel pears, core, and cut into ¼-inch-thick slices. Toss with remaining ½ teaspoon lemon juice.

Position rack in lower third of oven and preheat to 425°F. Spread chestnut filling evenly over bottom of cooled crust. Arrange apple and pear slices decoratively over filling. Drizzle with sweetener and margarine. Sprinkle with cinnamon. Bake tart 10 minutes. Reduce oven temperature to 350°F and bake until lightly browned, about 25 to 30 minutes. Serve warm or at room temperature.

VARIATIONS:

Substitute ½ teaspoon ground ginger for lemon peel in tart crust or substitute Linzertorte pastry (page 94).

❖ *HAWAIIAN PINEAPPLE–COCONUT TART* ❖

This is rich, but a sensation for special occasions.

MAKES ONE 9-INCH TART

COCONUT CRUST:

2 cups freshly grated coconut

¼ cup (½ stick) margarine, melted
2 tablespoons ground macadamias, pine nuts, or almonds
2 tablespoons natural liquid sweetener
½ teaspoon vanilla extract
½ teaspoon grated lemon peel (optional)

FILLING:

½ cup water
3 tablespoons natural liquid sweetener
1 tablespoon margarine
1 teaspoon vanilla extract
1 teaspoon fresh lemon juice
½ teaspoon grated lemon peel
½ teaspoon ground cinnamon
1 small ripe fresh pineapple, peeled, cored, and cut into
   ½-inch-thick crosswise slices (about eight 3-inch circles)

½ cup Basic Creme Pie filling (page 72)
   Toasted coconut and/or chopped nuts (optional
   garnishes)

For crust: Preheat oven to 400°F. Lightly grease rimmed baking sheet. Spread coconut evenly on sheet. Bake, stirring once or twice, until lightly and evenly browned, about 5 to 8 minutes. Let cool. Transfer to medium-size bowl.

Combine margarine, ground nuts, sweetener, vanilla, and lemon peel in small saucepan and place over low heat until bubbly, stirring frequently. Pour over coconut and toss to moisten evenly. Press mixture into tart pan. Chill at least 1 hour, or until firm.

For filling: Combine water, sweetener, margarine, vanilla, lemon juice and peel, and cinnamon in large heavy skillet and bring to boil over medium heat, stirring frequently. Add pineapple slices along with any accumulated juices and cook until liquid is reduced and slightly thickened, about 6 to 8 minutes. Remove from heat and let pineapple cool in syrup.

Preheat oven to 425°F. Spread creme pie filling or fruit puree evenly over bottom of crust. Arrange pineapple slices decoratively over filling, overlapping if necessary. Drizzle syrup over. Bake tart 15 minutes. Reduce oven temperature to 350°F and bake until pineapple is tender, about 30 minutes. Garnish with coconut or nuts if desired. Chill tart until serving time.

❖ LEMONY ORANGE CUSTARD TART ❖

MAKES ONE 9-INCH TART

½ cup water
¼ cup natural liquid sweetener
2 tablespoons fresh lemon juice
1 teaspoon vanilla extract
½ teaspoon grated lemon peel
3 large navel oranges, peeled and cut crosswise into
  ¼-inch-thick slices

Pastry Creme (page 84)
Basic Whole Wheat Tart Crust (page 83), baked
(substitute chilled fresh orange juice for water and add
½ teaspoon grated orange peel)
Fruit Glaze, made with apricots (page 85)

Combine water, sweetener, lemon juice, vanilla, and lemon peel in heavy large skillet and bring to boil over medium-high heat. Reduce heat to medium-low and simmer 5 minutes. Add orange slices and simmer until liquid is reduced and slightly thickened. Remove from heat and let orange slices cool in syrup.

Spread pastry creme evenly over bottom of cooled crust. Arrange orange slices decoratively over creme. Heat apricot glaze (adding remaining orange syrup if desired) and brush over oranges. Chill tart until serving time.

❖ *FRANGIPANE–PEAR TART* ❖

MAKES ONE 9-INCH TART OR TWO 4½-INCH TARTLETS

FRANGIPANE FILLING:

1 cup finely ground blanched almonds
9 tablespoons (1 stick plus 1 tablespoon) margarine
¼ cup soy milk
1½ tablespoons unbleached all-purpose flour or 1½ teaspoons arrowroot
1 teaspoon grated lemon peel
¼ teaspoon almond extract or ½ teaspoon vanilla extract
2 tablespoons natural liquid sweetener
1 teaspoon fresh lemon juice
1 teaspoon vanilla extract
5 medium-size ripe pears, peeled, cored, and cut into ¼-inch-thick slices

Basic Whole Wheat Tart Crust (page 83)
Apple Glaze (page 122) or Maple Glaze (page 179) or 2 tablespoons date sugar (optional garnishes)

Combine ground almonds, 6 tablespoons margarine, soy milk, flour or arrowroot, lemon peel, and almond extract (or ½ teaspoon vanilla) in food processor fitted with steel blade or blender and blend until thick and smooth. Set aside.

Combine remaining margarine, sweetener, lemon juice, and vanilla in large skillet and bring to boil over medium-high heat. Add pear slices, reduce heat to medium-low, and cook until pears are tender, about 8 to 10 minutes, turning occasionally. Let cool.

Position rack in lower third of oven and preheat to 400°F. Spread almond mixture evenly in crust. Arrange pear slices decoratively over filling. Drizzle with any remaining syrup. Bake 10 minutes. Reduce heat to 350°F and bake until pears are translucent and glazed, about 25 minutes longer. Brush with fruit glaze (see recipe for Ambrosia Fruit Tarts, page 85) or sprinkle with date sugar if desired. Serve at room temperature.

VARIATIONS:

Substitute apricots, peaches, or apples for pears.

❖ CAROB–TANGERINE TART ❖

MAKES ONE 9-INCH TART

¾ cup natural liquid sweetener
1 tablespoon corn oil or margarine
2 teaspoons vanilla extract
½ cup unsweetened carob powder, lightly toasted
3 tablespoons liquid (soy milk, unsweetened fruit juice, grain coffee substitute, or decaffeinated coffee)
   Basic Whole Wheat Tart Crust (page 83), baked, or Graham Cracker (or cookie crumb) Crust (page 63), well chilled
6 tangerines
½ cup fresh orange juice or water
   Creamy Soy Whip (page 173) (optional garnish)

Combine ½ cup sweetener, oil or margarine, and 1 teaspoon vanilla in medium-size saucepan and place over medium heat until heated through. Add carob powder and stir until smooth. Blend in liquid and simmer until mixture is thickened, about 3 to 4 minutes. Remove from heat and let cool to lukewarm. Spread filling evenly over bottom of crust; refrigerate.

Peel tangerines and separate sections, using tip of paring knife to remove any seeds. Place sections in medium-size saucepan. Add orange juice or water, remaining sweetener, and remaining vanilla and bring to boil over medium-high heat. Reduce heat and simmer until liquid thickens to form syrup. Remove from heat and let tangerine sections cool in syrup.

Arrange tangerine sections decoratively over filling. Use any remaining syrup to brush over sections to glaze, or mix into soy whip and pipe in rosettes around edge of tart. Chill until serving time.

❖ *UPSIDE-DOWN FRESH FRUIT TART* ❖

Any fresh seasonal fruit can be used—or try a creative assortment for still more flavor and color.

MAKES ONE 9-INCH TART

---

6 large baking apples *or* 8 ripe pears or other ripe fruits, peeled, cored, and cut into thick slices
1 teaspoon fresh lemon juice
½ cup natural liquid sweetener
1 teaspoon vanilla extract
½ teaspoon ground cinnamon
¼ teaspoon apple pie spice
¼ cup raisins, dried currants, or chopped nuts (optional)

¼ cup (½ stick) vegetable or soy margarine, melted

Pastry for Basic Whole Wheat Tart Crust (page 83), well chilled

---

Place fruit in large bowl. Sprinkle with lemon juice. Add ¼ cup sweetener along with vanilla and spices and toss to coat. Add raisins, currants, or nuts if desired.

Position rack in center of oven and preheat to 425°F. Grease deep 9-inch round pan; spoon in fruit mixture. Drizzle evenly with remaining sweetener and melted margarine.

Roll pastry out on lightly floured surface into 9-inch circle. Place pastry over fruit and press edges lightly against sides of pan. Slash crust in several places with knife to let steam escape. Bake 10 minutes. Reduce oven temperature to 375°F and bake until golden, about 30 minutes longer.

Let tart cool 10 minutes. Loosen edges gently with knife and invert onto serving plate. Serve warm.

❖ CAROB–WALNUT TART ❖

A traditional nut tart with a decadently delicious mocha twist.

MAKES ONE 8- TO 9-INCH TART

⅓ cup natural liquid sweetener
1½ tablespoons vegetable or soy margarine, melted and cooled
1 tablespoon blackstrap molasses
1½ teaspoons liquid lecithin
½ teaspoon vanilla extract
½ cup grain coffee substitute or decaffeinated coffee
1½ teaspoons arrowroot or ½ teaspoon kuzu powder
½ teaspoon ground cinnamon
Pinch of freshly grated nutmeg
½ cup coarsely chopped walnuts

Carob Glaze (page 44)
Basic Whole Wheat Tart Crust (page 83), partially baked (omit lemon peel; add 1 tablespoon lightly toasted unsweetened carob powder, page 64, to dry ingredients)

Position rack in lower third of oven and preheat to 425°F. Combine sweetener, margarine, molasses, lecithin, and vanilla in food processor fitted with steel blade or electric mixer bowl and blend until smooth and thickened. Combine coffee and arrowroot or kuzu. Add to molasses mixture along with spices and blend well. Stir in walnuts.

Spread ½-inch-thick layer of carob glaze over bottom of cooled crust. Top with nut mixture. Bake 15 minutes. Reduce oven temperature to 350°F and bake until center of filling is bubbly, about 25 to 30 minutes longer. Serve tart warm or at room temperature.

❖ *LINZERTORTE* ❖

This rich Austrian pastry is traditionally filled with raspberry preserves, but any fruit puree or preserves will do. The original recipe calls for eggs and butter, which are excluded here—but without sacrificing luscious flavor.

MAKES ONE 8-INCH DEEP DISH OR 9-INCH TART

1¾ cups whole wheat pastry flour
¾ cup finely ground almonds, toasted
2 tablespoons unsweetened carob powder, lightly toasted (see note, p. 64)
1 heaping teaspoon grated lemon peel
1 teaspoon arrowroot
1 teaspoon ground cinnamon
⅛ teaspoon ground cloves
3 tablespoons natural liquid sweetener
1¾ cups (3½ sticks) margarine, chilled and cut into 1-inch pieces
¼ cup grain coffee substitute or decaffeinated coffee, chilled
1 teaspoon vanilla extract

12 ounces fruit preserves or puree (preferably raspberry, apple, or apricot)
Soy milk or natural liquid sweetener to glaze (optional)

Combine flour, almonds, carob powder, lemon peel, arrowroot, and spices in food processor fitted with steel blade or in mixing bowl and blend well. Drizzle in sweetener and mix briefly. Cut in margarine until mixture resembles coarse crumbs. Add coffee and vanilla and blend just until dough holds together; do not overmix. Form into two equal balls and wrap in waxed paper or plastic. Flatten dough into discs and chill at least 2 hours.

Position rack in lower third of oven and preheat to 425°F. Lightly grease tart pan. Gently press half of dough into tart pan to thickness of about ¼ inch (dough can also be rolled out on lightly floured surface or between sheets of waxed paper). Prick all over with fork. Place in oven until partially baked, about 12 to 15 minutes. Let cool. Reduce oven temperature to 350°F.

Spread crust evenly with preserves. Roll out remaining dough to size of tart pan and cut into ½-inch-wide strips. Arrange in diagonal lattice over preserves, crimping edge to seal. Bake until golden, about 25 to 30 minutes. To glaze lattice, brush lightly with soy milk during last few minutes of baking, or brush warm tart with sweetener. Serve at room temperature.

VARIATIONS:
Linzertorte pastry is a perfect complement to many pie and tart fillings. For the thick layer of preserves, try substituting a thin layer of preserves or nut butter topped with poached fruit. Any extra dough can be cut with cookie cutters; sandwich the cookies with fruit puree or preserves.

❖ *FAVORITE FILLED TARTLETS* ❖

These melt-in-the-mouth dessert treats are a great way to use up leftover pastry or fillings. For extra crispness (and calories) try deep-frying rather than baking them; use oil preheated to 375°F. Tarts can be made up to 2 weeks ahead and frozen.

MAKES ABOUT 2 DOZEN 3-INCH TARTS

FILLING 1:
1 cup coarsely chopped nuts
¼ cup chopped raisins, dried currants, or other unsulfured dried fruit (optional)
3 tablespoons applesauce, fruit puree, or preserves
1 teaspoon ground cinnamon
½ teaspoon grated lemon peel
¼ teaspoon ground ginger

FILLING 2, CHESTNUT-CAROB CHIP FILLING:
Chestnut Creme Filling (page 72)
½ to ¾ cup unsweetened carob chips
1 teaspoon vanilla extract
¼ teaspoon ground cinnamon

FILLING 3:
Rice Creme (page 171), or cooked oatmeal
¼ cup chopped raisins (if not already in pudding)
2 tablespoons finely chopped pistachios (optional)
1 teaspoon rose water (see note, p. 96)
½ teaspoon grated lemon or orange peel
3 cardamom seeds, finely crushed

Pastry for one-crust pie or tart, well chilled
Soy milk

For filling: Combine all ingredients for any one of fillings and blend well.

Position rack in lower third of oven and preheat to 425°F. Roll pastry dough out on lightly floured surface to thickness of ¼ inch. Cut into 3-inch rounds, rerolling scraps as necessary. Place 1 heaping teaspoon filling mixture in center of half of rounds. Brush edges lightly with water. Top with remaining rounds, pressing edges to seal. Flatten slightly with rolling pin or palm of hand. Prick tops with fork to allow steam to escape. Brush lightly with soy milk. Arrange on baking sheets and bake until lightly browned, about 15 minutes. Serve warm or at room temperature.

NOTE: *Rose water can be purchased in gourmet food shops and health food stores.*

MISCELLANEOUS TARTS

Leftover pie or tart fillings, especially those that are not very thick, can be spooned into baked tartlet shells formed in muffin pans. Grease muffin cups and ease in pastry. Prick lightly with fork. Bake in lower third of preheated 425°F oven until lightly browned, about 10 to 15 minutes. Tartlet shells can also be partially baked, filled, and then baked at 350°F until filling is set.

ADDITIONAL WAYS TO USE PASTRY DOUGH

For turnovers: Cut pastry into 3-inch rounds or squares. Place 1 teaspoon filling in center of each. Brush edge of dough lightly with water, fold over, and press edges to seal. Prick tops with fork. Arrange on baking sheets and bake in lower third of preheated 425°F oven until lightly browned, about 15 minutes.

For horns or cornucopias: Cut pastry into 8-inch-long strips. Lightly grease metal cornucopia forms (available at specialty cookware shops). Roll dough strips around forms starting at pointed end and overlapping as you go. Chill thoroughly. Arrange on baking sheets. Bake in lower third of preheated 425°F oven until lightly browned, about 10 to 15 minutes, brushing lightly with soy milk during last few minutes of baking to glaze if desired. Remove from forms while warm and let cool completely on racks. Fill with Chestnut–Carob Chip Filling (page 95) or flavored Creamy Tofu Cheese Filling (page 175).

PUFF PASTRY

This rich pastry is the basis of many classic French desserts. It may take some practice to master what some consider the ultimate in *leâtisserie*, but the effort is well worth it. The secret to success lies in the distribution of fat in flour, with trapped air creating a light-textured, delicate product.

TIPS FOR SUCCESSFUL PUFF PASTRY

- Do not attempt to make pastry on a hot, humid, or rainy day.
- Although margarine should be chilled, it should not be too hard or it may break through the dough, releasing trapped air; it is the air between the dough and fat layers that causes the pastry to rise and expand. On the other hand, if margarine is too soft it will be absorbed into the flour, which will make the pastry heavy.
- Working pastry on a cold marble slab helps keep the margarine from softening while the dough is being rolled and shaped. If possible, chill the marble in the refrigerator before using.
- When cutting dough, always use a sharp knife or cutter so that the dough edges are not pressed together, which would keep the pastry from rising evenly. Placing cut pastry shapes floured side up on the baking sheet also helps assure an even rise.
- Do not stretch or pull the pastry while rolling or cutting it.
- Bake pastry on a baking sheet lined with parchment paper. If it begins to brown too quickly, cover with a second sheet of parchment.
- Pastry can be made ahead, filled (if desired), and frozen up to 2 weeks. Bake it straight from the freezer, allowing an additional 20 minutes oven time.

- Scraps and leftover strips of dough can be rerolled, but the result will not be quite as light and flaky. Use fancy cutters to make hearts, diamonds, fluted rounds, or squares. Brush with soy milk/sweetener and dust with cinnamon or date sugar. Bake as directed or freeze for later use.

❖ *WHOLE WHEAT PUFF PASTRY* ❖

Traditional puff pastry recipes call for high gluten flour, which forms a very elastic dough that will hold air bubbles. This recipe uses whole wheat pastry flour and a short-cut method: The result is a dough that, though more fragile to handle, does not need as much handling as a classic recipe would. A food processor is a time-saver here, but it must be used carefully to prevent the dough from toughening.

---

3 cups whole wheat pastry flour
¼ teaspoon salt (optional)
¾ cup (1½ sticks) margarine, chilled and cut into 1-inch pieces
¾ cup ice water

Combine flour and salt in food processor fitted with steel blade or in large bowl. Cut in half of margarine until mixture resembles coarse crumbs. If using processor, sprinkle ice water evenly over surface and process just until blended, about 3 seconds. If mixing by hand, make well in center of flour mixture. Pour in water all at once and stir with fork briskly but gently until evenly moistened. Form dough into ball. Wrap in waxed paper or plastic and chill 30 minutes.

Unwrap dough and transfer to lightly floured surface (a marble slab, which stays cool, is ideal). Cover with bowl or cloth and let rest a few minutes.

Knead 2 minutes to
develop elasticity.

Roll dough out into
½-inch-thick rectangle
about 12 by 6 inches.

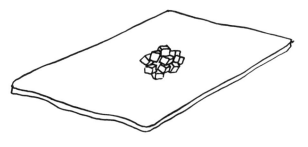

Place remaining pieces
of chilled margarine
in center of rectangle.

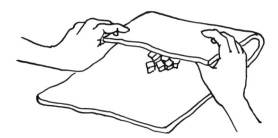

Fold one end over
to cover margarine,

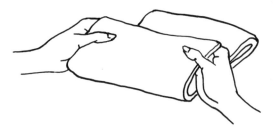

then fold opposite end
to cover first (for a total of
three layers of dough).

Pinch edges to seal. Wrap in waxed paper and chill 30 minutes.

Unwrap dough and return to lightly floured surface.

Roll into ½-inch-thick rectangle
of about the same
dimensions as before,

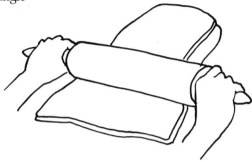

handling dough gently so that margarine does not break through. Check frequently to be sure dough is not sticking to work surface; flour lightly if necessary. Fold into thirds as before. Reroll into another rectangle slightly longer than before. Fold into thirds. Pinch edges to seal. Wrap in waxed paper and chill 30 minutes.

Repeat rolling and folding four more times, wrapping and chilling dough after first two times. Wrap and chill up to four days before shaping and baking.

❖ PETITE PASTRY SHELLS ❖

MAKES ABOUT 1½ DOZEN 3-INCH SHELLS

1. Use half of Whole Wheat Puff Pastry dough (page 99), reserving remainder for another use.
2. Roll pastry out on lightly floured surface (preferably a pastry cloth) into 10-by-16-inch rectangle about ¼ inch thick. Cut thirty-six circles in pastry using lightly floured 2-inch round cutter. Use smaller floured cutter to cut centers out of half of circles to make rings. Brush whole circles lightly with water and place one ring on each, pressing together gently. *Lightly* set small center cutouts back inside rings. Arrange shells on baking sheet lined with parchment paper. Cover lightly with waxed paper and chill at least 30 minutes. *(instructions continue)*

3. Preheat oven to 450°F. Remove waxed paper. Bake shells 7 minutes. Reduce oven temperature to 400°F and bake until shells are lightly browned, about 20 minutes, brushing tops with a mixture of 1 teaspoon soy milk and 1 teaspoon natural liquid sweetener during last few minutes of baking to glaze if desired. Transfer to racks to cool.

4. When completely cooled, lift out small "lids." Fill shells with Pastry Creme (page 84) and fresh fruit, or use any desired pie or tart filling. Dust lids with date sugar or cinnamon and set back into filling.

❖ *FLAN OR TART CASE (VOL-AU-VENT)* ❖

MAKES ONE 9-INCH TART SHELL

1. Use half of Whole Wheat Puff Pastry dough (page 99), reserving remainder for another use.

2. Roll pastry out on lightly floured surface (preferably a pastry cloth) into 10-by-16-inch rectangle about ¼ inch thick.

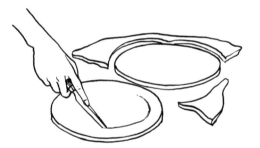

Using sharp knife, cut pastry into two 8-inch circles. Cut center out of one circle, leaving 1½-inch-wide ring.

(The dough of the remaining 5-inch center circle can be cut with fancy cutters or made into turnovers.)

3. Turn 8-inch circle floured side up. Transfer to baking sheet lined with parchment paper. Brush edges of circle lightly with water. Set pastry ring on top, floured side up.

Using sharp knife, make diagonal slashes vertically around edge (these are not only decorative, but help assure an even rise). Cover lightly with waxed paper and chill at least 30 minutes.

4. Preheat oven to 450°F. Remove waxed paper. Bake shell 7 minutes. Reduce oven temperature to 400°F and bake until lightly browned, about 25 minutes, brushing top edge with a mixture of 1 teaspoon soy milk and 1 teaspoon natural liquid sweetener during last few minutes of baking to glaze if desired. Transfer to rack to cool.

5. Fill with Pastry Creme (page 84) and fresh fruit, or use any desired pie or tart filling.

❖ *CORNUCOPIAS* ❖

These delicate cone-shaped pastries can be filled with flavored Soy Whip (page 173), a favorite "cheesecake" filling such as for Basic Creme Pie Filling and variations (page 72), or Creamy Tofu Cheese Filling (page 175) or Frangipane Filling (page 90)—use your imagination! They can be shaped on a standard-size cornet (available in specialty kitchenware stores) or rolled around any lightly greased tube or dowel. I have, on occasion, used large pastry tube tips to make miniature cones, to be filled and used for a special birthday cake decoration.

MAKES 1 DOZEN STANDARD-SIZE CONES

1. Use half of Whole Wheat Puff Pastry dough (page 99), reserving remainder for another use.

2. Roll pastry out on lightly floured surface (preferably a pastry cloth) into 12-inch square about ⅛ inch thick.

Using sharp knife or unfluted pastry wheel and straightedge as guide, cut twelve 1-inch strips of pastry.

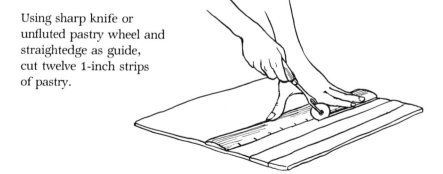

(instructions continue)

Transfer to baking sheet. Cover lightly with waxed paper and chill at least 20 minutes.

3. Lightly grease cornet forms. Remove only a few pastry strips at a time, keeping remainder refrigerated. Lightly brush one strip with water.

Roll around cornet starting at pointed end, with floured side of strip facing cornet and moistened side out, overlapping slightly with each turn. Pinch point of pastry to seal. Stop rolling ½ inch from wide end of cornet, cutting off any excess pastry, and press end against spiral to seal.

Place sealed side down on baking sheet lined with parchment paper. Repeat with remaining cones. Chill thoroughly.

4. Position rack in center of oven and preheat to 450°F. Brush tops of cones with a mixture of 1 teaspoon soy milk and 1 teaspoon natural liquid sweetener. Bake 7 minutes. Reduce oven temperature to 375°F and bake until golden, about 20 minutes.

5. Remove cones from oven. Gently slide off cornets. Return pastries to oven until insides are completely baked, about 15 minutes more. Transfer to racks to cool.

6. When completely cooled, spoon in desired filling and serve.

❖ FILLED CAKE ❖

MAKES ONE 8-INCH PASTRY

1. Use half of Whole Wheat Puff Pastry dough (page 99), reserving remainder for another use.

2. Roll pastry out on lightly floured surface (preferably a pastry cloth) into 9-by-16-inch rectangle about ⅜ inch thick. Using sharp knife, cut pastry into two 8-inch circles.

3. Turn floured side up. Transfer to baking sheets lined with parchment paper. Cover lightly with waxed paper and chill.

4. Prepare Frangipane Filling (page 90) or Vanilla Soy Cake Frosting (page 172). Shape filling into 4-inch round. Chill at least 45 minutes.

5. Remove waxed paper from pastry. Place filling in center of one pastry circle. Brush edges of pastry lightly with water. Use fluted pastry wheel to cut decorative design partially through remaining circle. Cut small hole in center of top, to allow steam to escape during cooking. Gently set atop filling, decorative side up, and press pastry edges together. Cut diagonal slashes vertically around edge of pastry as for Vol-au-Vent (page 147).

6. Preheat oven to 450°F. Bake 10 minutes. Reduce oven temperature to 375°F and bake until golden brown, about 40 minutes, brushing top with a mixture of 1 teaspoon soy milk and 1 teaspoon natural liquid sweetener during last 5 minutes of baking to glaze if desired. Serve at room temperature.

❖ NAPOLEONS ❖

Traditionally, this decadently rich pastry calls for custard-filled layers frosted with white sugar glaze and chocolate. This version substitutes a soy pastry creme sans cholesterol and excessive calories.

MAKES ABOUT 1½ DOZEN BARS

½ recipe Whole Wheat Puff Pastry (page 99)
1 recipe Pastry Creme (page 84) (can be flavored with
   grain coffee substitute, carob powder, or unsweetened
   fruit juice)
   Carob Glaze (page 128)

1. Divide puff pastry into thirds. Roll out each portion on lightly floured surface (preferably a pastry cloth) into 12-by-14-inch rectangle about ⅛ inch thick.

2. Turn floured side up. Transfer to baking sheets lined with parchment paper. Cover lightly with waxed paper and chill.

3. Preheat oven to 450°F. Prepare pastry creme; chill.

4. Remove waxed paper from pastry. Prick pastry all over with fork. Bake, one rectangle at a time, 7 minutes. Reduce oven temperature to 400°F and continue baking until lightly browned, about 20 minutes. Transfer to racks to cool.

5. When completely cooled, spread one layer with pastry creme; top with second layer. Again spread with creme; top with third layer.

6. Drizzle lightly with carob glaze and, if desired, with caramel. Refrigerate until chilled through, about 1 hour. Cut into bars with sharp knife.

NOTE: *If you wish, you may bake two of the rectangles at the same time. Place baking sheets on racks adjusted to the upper third and lower third of your oven. To insure even baking, about halfway through the baking time switch the rectangles from the top to the bottom rack (and vice versa) and continue baking.*

∴ POACHED FRUIT IN PASTRY ∴

MAKES 10 SERVINGS

½ recipe Whole Wheat Puff Pastry (page 99)
10 poached apples, pears, or peaches, cooled
   Fruit Glaze, see recipe for Ambrosia Fruit tarts (page 85) or Real Vanilla Bean Ice Creme (page 210)

1. Roll pastry out on lightly floured surface (preferably a pastry cloth) to thickness of ¼ inch. Using sharp knife, cut into squares large enough that each will completely enclose one fruit. Set one fruit on center of one square and lift edges, pressing together atop fruit to seal. Repeat with remaining pastry and fruit. Cut small leaves or decorative shapes from pastry scraps, brush lightly with water, and press into pastry casings. Arrange on baking sheets lined with parchment paper and chill at least 30 minutes.

2. Position rack in center of oven and preheat to 450°F. Brush pastry with soy milk-sweetener mixture. Bake 10 minutes. Reduce oven temperature to 375°F and bake until golden, about 25 minutes more.

3. Serve warm, drizzled with glaze or accompanied with vanilla bean ice creme.

·:· *PETITE PALMIERS* ·:·

1. Roll pastry out on lightly floured surface (preferably a pastry cloth) into long rectangle 8 inches wide and ⅛ inch thick. Fold one long edge three times to center of rectangle,

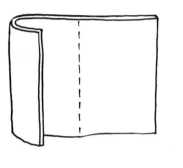 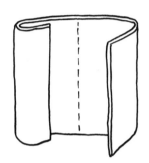

then fold in other long edge three times to meet first.

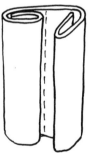

Then fold the halves together.

Wrap pastry in waxed paper and chill at least 45 minutes.

(instructions continue)

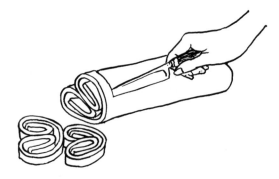

2. Using sharp knife, cut pastry into ¼-inch-thick slices.

Place on baking sheet lined with parchment paper and chill thoroughly.

3. Preheat oven to 450°F. Bake palmiers 7 minutes. Reduce oven temperature to 400°F and bake until golden, about 20 minutes, brushing with natural liquid sweetener during last few minutes of baking to glaze if desired. Transfer to racks to cool.

•:• *PINWHEELS* •:•

1. Roll pastry out on lightly floured surface (preferably a pastry cloth) into ⅛-inch-thick rectangle. Spread with mixture of chopped raisins or dried currants, cinnamon, vanilla, and enough fruit puree or nut butter to bind. Roll up as for jelly roll, pinching end to seal. Using sharp knife, cut roll into ⅜-inch-thick slices. Arrange on baking sheet lined with parchment paper and chill at least 30 minutes.

2. Preheat oven to 450°F. Brush pastry with mixture of 1 teaspoon soy milk and 1 teaspoon natural liquid sweetener. Bake 7 minutes. Reduce oven temperature to 375°F and bake until golden, about 20 minutes more. Serve warm or at room temperature.

❖ *TURNOVERS* ❖

This is a delicious way to utilize scraps of leftover pastry; however, keep in mind that rerolled puff pastry loses some of its rising ability and will not be quite as flaky and light in texture.

1. Roll pastry out on lightly floured surface (preferably a pastry cloth) to thickness of ¼ inch. Cut to desired size with floured round or square cutters.

2. Spread about 1 tablespoon (depending on size of pastry shapes) preserves, applesauce, or other cooked fruit filling in center of pastry pieces. Fold in half to form semicircles or triangles; press edges with fork to seal. Arrange on baking sheet lined with parchment paper and chill at least 30 minutes.

3. Preheat oven to 450°F. Brush tops of turnovers with a mixture of 1 teaspoon soy milk and 1 teaspoon natural liquid sweetener. Bake 7 minutes. Reduce oven temperature to 375°F and bake until golden, about 20 minutes more. Serve warm or at room temperature.

VARIATION:

Use fancy cutters to cut even number of each shape. Prick cut shapes all over with fork. Chill and bake as directed for turnovers; let cool. When completely cooled, spread one of each shape with small amount of preserves, Pastry Creme (page 84), or other creme filling; top with remaining pastry. Drizzle tops with Carob Glaze (page 128) if desired, and/or sprinkle with finely chopped nuts or date sugar.

Cakes

Cakes of all shapes, sizes, and flavors are fondly associated with many festive occasions. Cakes that are candle-lit, ornate, or simple–everyone has a favorite!

It's a rewarding feeling to serve a cake made from scratch, but unfortunately, with convenience a top priority in most households, cakes made from mixes have come to be considered homemade. The following cake recipes were developed with speed and simplicity in mind. An easily accessible electric mixer or food processor is a great time and energy saver that can mix a cake or whip a filling in minutes.

Many of these recipes have been fashioned after such American favorites as carrot cake, applesauce spice cake, Boston cream pie, and chocolate layer cake. The variations included after each recipe offer exciting taste twists—or create your own, using a basic cake with one of the numerous fillings and decorating ideas.

STEPS TO SUCCESS
(so cakes don't have to wait for special occasions!)

MEASURING AND MIXING

- Read the entire recipe before beginning. Assemble all the ingredients and equipment, including the greased baking pan, before measuring and mixing.
- If you grease baking pans with lightly warmed liquid lecithin (available at most health food stores), it's not necessary to flour. Margarine can also be used to grease; in this case the pan should be lightly floured. Since cakes made with liquid sweeteners tend to bake faster on the outside than the inside, it's a good idea to line bottoms of cake pans with a circle of lightly greased waxed paper or parchment to prevent burning.
- If baker's yeast is being used as a leavener, it should be proofed to make sure it's active before mixing it with the other ingredients.

- It's not necessary to sift whole-grain flours for other baked desserts, but in cake making sifting helps ensure a lighter texture. The flour can be sifted and the bran stirred back in, or save the bran and add it to cookie or muffin batters.
- An electric mixer or food processor is a real asset; the air incorporated into the batter results in a lighter cake. But be careful not to overbeat the batter after the flour is added or the cake will be heavy.
- The measures given are as accurate as possible, but various whole-grain flours absorb liquids differently and sweetener syrups also vary in consistency. If baker's yeast is used instead of baking powder, this will cause another variation in consistency. Most cake batters should pour freely from the mixing bowl unless stated otherwise (fruit cakes, for example have a heavier batter). Yeast-leavened cake batters should be soft, light, and spongy. Follow this basic procedure for preparing cakes unless otherwise specified in the recipe:

    1. Whip the shortening and sweetener together with a wire whisk or in a food processor or electric mixer until creamy and syrupy.

    2. Sift the dry ingredients together into another bowl. Blend the remaining wet ingredients separately. Alternately add the dry and wet ingredients to the creamed shortening/sweetener mixture. When using an electric mixer—and especially a food processor—*be careful not to overbeat* or the flour will develop too much gluten and the cake will be heavy.

    3. Dried fruits, nuts, or fresh fruits are usually stirred in last.

    4. When increasing or decreasing sweetener, remember to adjust other liquids in the recipe if the change is by more than 2 tablespoons.

    5. Always try to end mixing with dry ingredients.

A WORD ABOUT INGREDIENTS:

FLOURS AND GRAINS

- For light cakes use pastry flour made from soft whole wheat (hard wheat flour is best for breads and cookies). Most well-stocked natural foods stores carry both soft and hard wheat flour.

- Save stale bread pieces to make fine bread crumbs. Up to ¼ cup flour can be replaced with bread crumbs, which helps to lighten texture.
- Adding cooked millet, couscous, or other grain also lightens cake texture. Use up to ¾ cup cooked grain in place of an equal quantity of flour; adjust the liquid if needed.
- Sweet brown rice flour, barley flour, and soy flour can replace ¼ to ½ cup of the wheat flour called for. (These flours do not contain enough gluten to be used alone.)

SWEETENING

- These recipes use as little sweetener as possible. If you find the batter needs more, add 1 to 2 tablespoonfuls before adding the last of the dry ingredients.

LEAVENING

- Baking soda has not been used in these recipes, as it is thought to deplete vitamins C and E and there are many effective alternative leavening agents. Baking powder contains a considerable smaller amount of bicarbonate (see following recipe for homemade baking powder using potassium instead of sodium bicarbonate, which reduces the salt content as well). If baking powder is store-bought, be sure it is aluminum-free. Baker's yeast is an excellent leavening agent for cakes, since it contains enzymes that break down the phytic acids found in whole grains and flours. Some cooks may shy away from using yeast, opting for the convenience of baking powder. Yeast is easy to use, but it does involve a longer preparation time since the cake must rise in the pan before baking. I have included a basic method for substituting yeast as a leavener in cakes when the recipe calls for baking powder (page 116).
- A leavening agent can be omitted altogether, but the cake will be heavier in texture. (If leavening is excluded, place a heat-proof bowl containing a small amount of water in the bottom of the oven during baking. This creates steam, which helps to lighten the cake and prevent the bottom and sides from burning.) If you use a fermented grain sweetener, such as barley malt or amasake, leaving the cake batter overnight in a warm place (such as an oven with pilot light only) may provide a

slight leavening effect. Unleavened cakes can also be baked in two or three pans (you may want to make extra batter) or split into layers after baking and filled for a higher effect.

❖ *HOMEMADE BAKING POWDER* ❖

This recipe uses potassium bicarbonate instead of sodium bicarbonate; purchase it from the druggist's counter in a pharmacy. Mix in small quantities and store in an airtight container.

---

1 part potassium bicarbonate
2 parts cream of tartar
2 parts arrowroot

Sift all ingredients together three times. substitute for equal measure of store-bought baking powder.

- *Baking with yeast:* Baker's yeast can be purchased in compressed cubes or as dry granules in premeasured packets or bulk form. I prefer to buy dry yeast from a natural foods store in bulk. The granules are easy to measure, keep well when stored properly, and are more economical, especially if you do a fair amount of baking. Unless noted in a particular recipe, 1 to 1½ tablespoons dry yeast granules are sufficient to give a nice rise to the cakes in this chapter. If you want to substitute yeast for the baking powder measures, you must first proof the yeast.
- *Proofing the yeast:* Place the following in a cup or small bowl: ½ cup warm water (slightly warmer than lukewarm but *not hot* or the live yeast will be killed); 1 tablespoon natural liquid sweetener (room temperature, not cold); and 1½ level tablespoons dry yeast granules (unless a different amount is specified in the recipe) *or* 1 cake compressed yeast (removed from the refrigerator at least 30 minutes before using). Stir to dissolve yeast. Set aside until mixture begins to bubble, about 10

minutes. If mixture does not bubble, then the yeast is not alive—either the liquid was too hot or the yeast too old.

• *Basic rising procedure:*

1. Combine the liquid, sweetener, and oil or melted margarine called for in the recipe in a large mixing bowl. Add the proofed yeast mixture and blend well.

2. Add the premeasured dry ingredients (flours, spices, and salt) and beat well to blend.

3. Cover the bowl with a cloth and set in a warm place, such as the oven with pilot light. Let rise until doubled in size. Beat in any nuts, raisins, dried fruits or grated peels called for in the recipe; if no additional ingredients are to be added, beat the plain batter for a few minutes.

4. Spoon the batter into the greased cake pan or pans, cover with a cloth, and set in a warm place. When the batter has risen almost three fourths up the sides of the pans, preheat the oven to the desired temperature.

5. Remove the cloth and bake the cake layers for the time suggested in the recipe. *Do not let batter rise higher than just under the top of the pan;* this results in a heavy-textured cake. If the batter is allowed to rise for too long, it may also taste too "yeasty."

FLAVORINGS AND ADDITIONS

• Nuts, raisins, and other dried fruits should be folded or stirred into the batter last—for both baking-powder- and yeast-risen batters. To keep these ingredients from sinking to the bottom, make sure they are at room temperature, and dust them lightly with a small amount of flour before stirring them into the batter. If raisins or dried fruits are extremely dry, soak them in any flavor extract called for, plus a little of the required liquid, for 15 minutes; squeeze out the liquid and use it in recipe.

• Adding ½ teaspoon of apple cider vinegar to batter helps insure a delicate crumb.

• Lightly toasting carob powder (see note, p. 64) enhances flavor and lends a more chocolaty taste.

• Lightly toasting soy flour improves digestibility and flavor.

BAKING CAKES

- Always preheat the oven at least 15 minutes before baking. Most of these recipes take no more than 20 minutes to mix, so the oven can be preheated when you begin.
- Suggested baking times are not always accurate, so check with a cake tester or knife close to finishing time. If the tester comes out clean, with no cake batter sticking to it, the cake is ready.
- Remove the cake from the oven when fully baked and let cool on a rack approximately 15 minutes. This allows air to circulate freely and uniformly around pan. Loosen the sides of the cake with a knife, place a cake rack over the top of the pan, and invert. Tap the bottom of the pan lightly and evenly to loosen the cake. The cake should fall easily from the pan, but if it is sticking, do not force it. Place the pan on a towel dampened with hot water for a few minutes and try again, making sure you have loosened the sides well with a knife. If the layer does break, try to piece it together while warm, using a small amount of thick filling to hold it together. (Chestnut filling is particularly good for this.)
- To ensure that the cake is moist outside as well as in, and to further meld flavors, wrap it in plastic or waxed paper while still barely warm from the oven. Leave at room temperature for several hours, or overnight if possible. Unwrap, fill, and glaze. The cake can also be frozen after being wrapped in plastic: Let cool thoroughly, wrap plastic-covered layers in foil, and freeze.
- No cake is a total failure (. . . well, almost). Too-heavy cakes can be cut into cubes, sprinkled with fruit juice, and served topped with fresh fruit. Leftover pieces can be dried in the oven and made into crumbs, which have many uses. Broken or uneven layers can be cut with fancy shapes and made into petits fours and tea cakes.

APPLE CAKES

I could almost fill a separate chapter with apple cake recipes. Every country, even every family, seems to have a traditional favorite. Here are the ones that made it through the ingredient changes sucessfully and deliciously!

❖ *QUICK AND EASY APPLESAUCE CAKE* ❖

MAKES ONE 9-INCH BUNDT CAKE

---

1 cup natural liquid sweetener
¾ cup corn oil
2½ cups whole wheat pastry flour
2 teaspoons baking powder
1½ teaspoons ground cinnamon
½ teaspoon ground cloves
½ teaspoon freshly grated nutmeg
½ teaspoon salt
1¾ cups unsweetened applesauce
1½ teaspoons vanilla extract
½ cup raisins or unsulfured dried currants
½ cup chopped pecans

Preheat oven to 350°F. Grease 9-inch bundt pan. Combine sweetener and oil in food processor fitted with steel blade or large bowl of electric mixer and blend until creamy and thickened. Sift together flour, baking powder, spices, and salt. Mix applesauce and vanilla and add to creamed mixture alternately with dry ingredients, ending with dry ingredients. Fold in raisins or currants and nuts. Turn into prepared pan. Bake until tester inserted near center comes out clean, about 50 to 60 minutes. Let cool on rack.

❖ *APPLESAUCE CAKE* ❖

This cake, made with soy flour, wheat germ, and yeast flakes, is super-nutritious. The batter can also be baked in muffin tins, providing a healthy treat for a snack or lunchbox.

MAKES ONE 9-INCH BUNDT CAKE OR TWO 9-INCH ROUND LAYERS

¾ cup natural liquid sweetener
½ cup corn oil
1½ cups whole wheat pastry flour
½ cup soy flour, lightly toasted
¼ cup unbleached all-purpose flour
2 teaspoons baking powder
½ teaspoon salt
2 teaspoons ground cinnamon
¼ teaspoon ground cloves
¼ teaspoon freshly grated nutmeg
1 cup unsweetened applesauce
½ cup wheat germ
2 tablespoons nutritional yeast flakes
½ to ¾ cup raisins

Preheat oven to 350°F. Grease 9-inch bundt pan or two 9-inch layer pans. Combine sweetener and oil in food processor fitted with steel blade or in large bowl of electric mixer and blend until creamy. Sift together flours, baking powder, salt, and spices. Stir applesauce into creamed mixture. Add sifted dry ingredients, wheat germ, and yeast flakes. If using food processor, blend one minute using on/off turns. If using electric mixer, beat about 3 minutes. Fold in raisins. Turn batter into prepared pan. Bake until tester inserted near center comes out clean, about 40 to 45 minutes. Let cool on rack. Wrap cooled cake in plastic and let stand overnight.

VARIATION:

Replace ¼ cup whole wheat flour with equal amount of rolled oats.

❖ *FRESH APPLE–PECAN CAKE* ❖

This large cake is great for a buffet brunch table—it will serve 12 to 16 people.

MAKES ONE 10-INCH TUBE CAKE

1¼ cups natural liquid sweetener

1 cup corn oil

2 teaspoons vanilla extract

2½ cups whole wheat pastry flour

2 teaspoons baking powder

1½ teaspoons ground cinnamon

½ teaspoon freshly grated nutmeg

½ teaspoon salt

3 cups peeled, cored, and diced tart apples, sprinkled with 1 teaspoon fresh lemon juice

¾ cup chopped pecans

½ cup raisins

Apple Glaze (see recipe) or maple syrup, warmed (optional)

Finely chopped pecans (optional garnish)

Preheat oven to 350°F. Grease and flour 10-inch tube pan. Combine sweetener and oil in food processor fitted with steel blade or in large bowl of electric mixer and blend until creamy. Beat in vanilla. Sift together dry ingredients. Add to creamed mixture and mix until evenly moistened. Stir in apples, pecans, and raisins (batter will be thick). Turn into prepared pan. Bake until tester inserted near center comes out clean, about 1½ hours.

Let cake cool in pan 15 minutes; invert onto serving plate. While still warm, brush with Apple Glaze or warmed maple syrup. Sprinkle top of cake with pecans if desired.

APPLE GLAZE

MAKES ABOUT ½ CUP

---

1 cup unfiltered apple juice or cider

½ teaspoon ground cinnamon (optional)

Simmer juice in small saucepan over medium heat until reduced by about half. Stir in cinnamon if desired.

❖ *APPLE BROWN BETTY* ❖

An adaptation of a simple but delicious American favorite. It's not exactly a cake, but as long as we're baking with apples . . .

MAKES ONE 8-INCH SQUARE PAN

FILLING:
- 3 cups peeled, cored, and sliced baking apples
- ¼ cup natural liquid sweetener
- ¼ cup raisins or unsulfured dried currants (optional)
- ¼ cup chopped nuts (optional)
- 1 teaspoon grated lemon peel
- 1 teaspoon fresh lemon juice
- 1 teaspoon ground cinnamon
- ¼ teaspoon freshly grated nutmeg

TOPPING:
- 2 cups whole wheat pastry flour
- ½ cup natural liquid sweetener
- ½ cup rolled oats
- ¼ cup corn oil
- 1 teaspoon ground cinnamon

Real Vanilla Bean Ice Creme (page 210) (optional garnish)

For filling: Preheat oven to 375°F. Grease 8-inch square pan. Mix all filling ingredients well and spread in prepared pan.

For topping: Combine all ingredients until evenly moistened. Sprinkle evenly over filling. Bake until topping is crisp and golden, about 30 to 35 minutes. Serve warm, topping with ice creme if desired.

VARIATIONS:

Substitute peeled and pitted fresh peaches, plums, or apricots for apples.

❖ *APPLE KUCHEN* ❖

A sweet, crumbly crust layered with apples (or other fresh fruit) and topped with an eggless creamy custard. So easy and so good—this recipe is one you can count on in a pinch.

MAKES ONE 13-BY-9-INCH KUCHEN

CRUST:

1¾ cups whole wheat pastry flour
 1 teaspoon ground cinnamon
 ½ teaspoon baking powder
 ½ teaspoon grated lemon peel
 ½ cup (1 stick) margarine, well chilled and cut into small pieces
 1 tablespoon natural liquid sweetener
 1 tablespoon soy milk or unsweetened fruit juice

FILLING:

 5 medium-large baking apples, peeled, cored, and sliced
⅔ cup natural liquid sweetener
 Fresh lemon juice
1½ teaspoons ground cinnamon
1½ teaspoons vanilla extract *or* 1 teaspoon vanilla plus ½ teaspoon natural brandy flavoring
 ½ cup raisins (optional)

TOPPING:

 1 cup soy milk
 1 tablespoon arrowroot or 1 teaspoon kuzu powder
 ½ teaspoon ground cinnamon (optional)
 ½ teaspoon vanilla extract

For crust: Grease 13-by-9-inch pan. Sift flour, cinnamon, and baking powder into food processor fitted with steel blade or into large bowl of electric mixer. Add lemon peel. Cut in margarine until mixture resembles small peas. Drizzle in sweetener and soy milk or fruit juice and blend just until mixture begins to hold together. Press into prepared pan and chill thoroughly.

For filling: Preheat oven to 375°F. Sprinkle apples with sweetener, lemon juice to taste, cinnamon, and flavoring. Toss in raisins if desired. Spread evenly over chilled crust.

For topping: Blend soy milk, arrowroot or kuzu, cinnamon, and vanilla. Pour evenly over apple mixture. Bake until golden, about 30 to 35 minutes. Serve kuchen warm.

VARIATIONS:

Substitute other fresh fruit for apples—berries are especially delicious.

Toss fruit with a fresh fruit puree or preserves; decrease sweetener to taste.

Substitute rolled oats or cookie crumbs for part of flour.

❖ *CHAMELEON CAKE* ❖

Don't worry—there are no lizards in this cake! It's a wonderfully easy recipe that lends itself to many delicious variations.

MAKES TWO 8-INCH LAYERS

¾ cup natural liquid sweetener
½ cup corn oil
2¾ cups whole wheat pastry flour
1½ teaspoons baking powder
¼ teaspoon salt
1¾ cups liquid (can be orange juice, powdered grain coffee substitute, soy milk, or water)
2 teaspoons vanilla
½ teaspoon apple cider vinegar

Preheat oven to 350°F. Grease and flour two 8-inch round pans. Combine sweetener and oil in food processor fitted with steel blade or in large bowl of electric mixer and blend until thickened and syrupy. Sift together dry ingredients. Combine liquid, vanilla, and vinegar.

Add dry and liquid ingredients alternately to oil mixture. Blend well but do not overbeat, especially if using food processor. Divide batter between prepared pans. Bake until tester inserted near center comes out clean, about 30 to 35 minutes. Let cool on racks. Fill and glaze cooled cake as desired, or cake can be frozen, then thawed and filled at a later date.

(recipe continues)

VARIATIONS:

Ambrosia Cake: Use rice or Amasake sweetener (page 166); replace up to ½ cup whole wheat pastry flour with equal amount of rice flour; use fresh coconut milk (if available) or soy milk for liquid. Add grated peel of one medium-size lemon or small orange. Fill with Fruit Glaze (page 85) and a layer of assorted sliced fresh fruit (for example, strawberries, peaches, bananas sprinkled with fresh lemon juice, kiwi); sprinkle fruit with toasted unsweetened coconut shreds. Glaze top of cake with strawberry preserves and sprinkle with additional coconut. This cake should be served the same day; otherwise, substitute poached fruit from the preparation of the Fruit Glaze and garnish each serving with sliced fresh fruit.

Florida Sunshine Cake: Sweeten with sorghum syrup if available. Use 1 cup fresh orange juice and ¼ cup each fresh lime juice, lemon juice, and water for required liquid. Add grated peel of one small lemon and ½ small lime. Bake as above. This is a very tangy cake that improves in flavor the second day.

Marble Swirl Cake: Prepare basic recipe for Chameleon Cake. Remove one third of batter and blend in ¼ cup unsweetened cocoa powder or lightly toasted unsweetened carob powder, 3 tablespoons natural liquid sweetener, and 3 tablespoons melted margarine. Turn white batter into well-greased 9-inch bundt pan or prepared 8-inch layer pans. Pour in chocolate batter in spiral fashion. Use knife to swirl batters together. Bake as above. If baked in layers, cake can be filled with Mocha Frosting, or Creamy Tofu-Carob Chip Filling (pages 170 and 148).

❖ *NUTTY CAROB CAKE* ❖

A rich, moist cake resembling brownies.

MAKES ONE 13-BY-9-INCH CAKE

¾ cup maple syrup or barley malt with corn syrup (see note, p. 128)
½ cup (1 stick) margarine
¾ cup unsweetened carob powder, lightly toasted
1 cup grain coffee substitute or decaffeinated coffee, lukewarm
1½ tablespoons vanilla extract
1 teaspoon apple cider vinegar
2¼ cups soft whole wheat pastry flour
2 teaspoons baking powder
1 teaspoon ground cinnamon
¾ cup chopped nuts (pecans, walnuts, hazelnuts, and/or almonds)

Carob Glaze (see recipe, p. 128) (optional)

Preheat oven to 350°F. Generously grease 13-by-9-inch pan. Combine maple syrup or barley malt and margarine in food processor fitted with steel blade or in large bowl of electric mixer and blend until creamy and thickened. Blend carob powder with small amount of coffee to form smooth paste. Add to creamed mixture.

Mix remaining coffee, vanilla, and vinegar. Sift together flour, baking powder, and cinnamon. Add liquid and dry ingredients alternately to creamed carob mixture, ending with dry ingredients; blend well but do not overbeat. Stir in nuts. Turn batter into prepared pan. Bake until tester inserted near center comes out clean, about 30 to 35 minutes.

VARIATION:

Replace 1½ cups whole wheat pastry flour with equal amount of chestnut or brown rice flour. Both flours provide a pleasing crunchy texture.

If desired, top with: *(recipe continues)*

CAROB GLAZE:

MAKES ABOUT 1 CUP

½ cup unsweetened carob powder
¾ cup natural liquid sweetener
½ teaspoon ground cinnamon
½ teaspoon vanilla extract

Lightly toast carob powder in small heavy skillet over medium-low heat. Add sweetener, cinnamon, and vanilla, reduce heat to low, and stir until mixture begins to bubble. Let bubble for 3 to 5 minutes; remove from heat. Let cool to lukewarm. Drizzle over cake while glaze is still warm. Any leftover glaze can be covered and refrigerated to serve over soy ice cream or tea breads, or used for brushing over bottoms of tart shells before filling.

NOTE: A mixture of barley malt and pure corn syrup can be purchased in health food stores.

❖ CARROT–SPICE CAKE ❖

Food, like clothing, is governed by fashions that go in and out of vogue, but the popularity of this moist cake has made it an American classic. This recipe adds a new twist to the standard ingredients, enriching both flavor and color.

MAKES ONE 13-BY-9-INCH CAKE OR TWO 8-INCH ROUND LAYERS

¾ cup natural liquid sweetener
¾ cup corn oil
2¼ cups whole wheat pastry flour
2¼ teaspoons baking powder
1½ teaspoons ground cinnamon
½ teaspoon salt
¼ teaspoon ground cloves
¼ teaspoon ground allspice
5 tablespoons V-8 or tomato juice
2¾ cups finely grated carrots
¾ cup raisins or other dried fruit (dried apricots and pineapple should be cooked and drained)

Vanilla Soy Cake Frosting (page 172) and toasted chopped nuts (optional for 13-by-9-inch cake)
Apricot- or pineapple-flavored Creamy Tofu Cheese Filling (page 175) (optional for 8-inch layers)

Preheat oven to 350°F. Generously grease one 13-by-9-inch or two 8-inch round pans. Combine sweetener and oil in food processor fitted with steel blade or in large bowl of electric mixer and blend until creamy. Sift together dry ingredients. Add to creamed mixture alternately with V-8 or tomato juice; blend well but do not overbeat. Stir in carrots and raisins or dried fruit (batter will be thick but not dry). Turn into prepared pan. Bake until tester inserted near center comes out clean, about 50 to 55 minutes. Let cool on rack. Wrap cooled cake in plastic, then foil. Let stand at room temperature overnight, if possible, before filling or glazing.

If desired, frost with soy frosting and toasted chopped nuts or fill with apricot or pineapple tofu cheese filling. *(recipe continues)*

VARIATIONS:

Replace ¼ cup flour with equal amount of lightly toasted unsweetened carob (see note, p. 64) or cocoa powder.

Use ½ cup raisins or dried fruit and ½ cup chopped nuts.

Replace ¾ cup of the grated carrots with ½ cup chopped fresh pineapple.

❖ *HONEY–SPICE CAKE* ❖

This moist cake is a favorite in my home—bake ahead, wrap, and store (or freeze) for at least a day before serving to meld flavors. It will stay moist and fresh for a week or more, if it lasts that long.

The cake doesn't need any topping, but can be garnished with finely chopped toasted almonds. Or, for special occasions, fill center with apricot-flavored Creamy Tofu Cheese Filling (page 175) and garnish with sliced fresh fruit.

MAKES ONE 9-INCH TUBE CAKE

½ cup (1 stick) margarine
⅓ cup raw light honey
⅓ cup natural liquid sweetener
1¾ cups of whole wheat pastry flour
2 teaspoons baking powder
½ teaspoon *each* ground cinnamon, ground ginger, allspice, and freshly grated nutmeg
½ cup (or more) grain coffee substitute or decaffeinated coffee
2 teaspoons vanilla extract
¼ cup chopped blanched almonds
¼ cup finely chopped orange peel (preferably from organically grown orange)
3 ounces mixed raisins and unsulfured pitted dates, finely chopped

---

Preheat oven to 350°F. Grease and flour 9-inch tube pan. Combine margarine and sweeteners in small saucepan and place over medium-low heat until margarine is melted. Remove from heat and let cool to lukewarm.

Sift together flour, baking powder, and spices into food processor fitted with steel blade or into large bowl of electric mixer. Add sweetener mixture, ½ cup coffee, and vanilla and blend well (do not overbeat), adding up to 2 more tablespoons coffee if batter seems too dry. Stir in chopped almonds, peel, raisins, and dates. Turn batter into prepared pan. Bake until tester inserted near center comes out clean, about 30 to 40 minutes. Let cool on rack. Wrap cooled cake in plastic and let stand overnight.

❖ *MOCHA–BANANA–POPPYSEED CAKE* ❖

Yes, this cake sounds and is a real mouthful! It's rich but not too sweet—a perfect cake for brunch. Chopped nuts and sliced bananas sprinkled with lemon juice make an excellent garnish.

MAKES ONE 9-INCH ROUND LAYERS

½ cup grain coffee substitute or decaffeinated coffee
3 tablespoons poppyseeds
1½ teaspoons vanilla extract
3 medium-size ripe bananas, peeled
½ teaspoon fresh lemon juice

¾ cup natural liquid sweetener
½ cup corn oil
2 cups whole wheat pastry flour *or* 1½ cups whole wheat pastry flour and ½ cup oat flour
2 teaspoons baking powder
1½ teaspoons ground cinnamon
¼ teaspoon freshly grated nutmeg
¼ teaspoon salt
½ cup chopped pecans or toasted chopped almonds (optional)
Lemon–Maple Glaze (page 179) or Vanilla Soy Cake Frosting (page 172) (optional)

Preheat oven to 350°F. Grease 9-inch bundt or two 9-inch round pans. Combine coffee and poppyseeds in small saucepan and bring to boil, then simmer over low heat 3 minutes. Remove from heat. Stir in vanilla and let cool. Mash bananas with lemon juice. Stir into cooled poppyseed mixture. *(recipe continues)*

Combine sweetener and oil in food processor fitted with steel blade or in large bowl of electric mixer and blend until creamy. Sift together dry ingredients. Add to creamed mixture alternately with bananas; blend well but do not overbeat. Stir in nuts if desired. Turn batter into prepared pans. Bake until tester inserted near center comes out clean, about 35 to 40 minutes. Let cool on rack. Wrap cooled cake in plastic and let stand overnight to meld flavors.

If desired, glaze with lemon–maple glaze or top with vanilla soy frosting.

VARIATIONS:

Replace ¼ cup flour with equal amount of lightly toasted unsweetened carob powder (see note, p. 64).

Use 2 medium-size ripe bananas and 4 ounces chopped fresh pineapple, replacing some or all of coffee with pineapple juice.

❖ *CHEESELESS CHEESECAKE* ❖

I had my first delicious taste of cheeseless cheesecake at the Farm in Tennessee almost ten years ago! Unlike cake made with eggs and dairy cheese, this is cholesterol-free and low calorie (depending on the choice of crust and topping). I love to serve these cheesecakes to unsuspecting guests—very few people even notice that they are made with tofu!

THIS RECIPE MAKES A LARGE (10-INCH SPRINGFORM) CHEESECAKE. TO BAKE IN
A 9-INCH SPRINGFORM, DECREASE INGREDIENTS BY ONE THIRD. FOR A 9-INCH
PIE PAN, DECREASE INGREDIENTS BY ONE HALF.

Graham Cracker (or cookie crumb) Crust (page 63)

    5 cups soft tofu
    1 cup natural liquid sweetener (a combination of
      maple and rice syrups is especially good)
    ½ cup corn oil
    2 teaspoons vanilla extract *or* seeds scraped from
      inside of 1-inch piece vanilla bean
    1 teaspoon fresh lemon juice
      Grated peel of 1 medium-size lemon
    ½ teaspoon salt (optional)
  ½ to ¾ cup soy milk

Lightly grease 10-inch springform pan. Pat crumb crust mixture on bottom and halfway up sides (crust should be about ¼ inch thick).

Preheat oven to 400°F. Combine tofu, sweetener, and oil in food processor fitted with steel blade or in blender and blend well. Mix in vanilla, lemon juice, grated peel, and salt. With machine running, gradually pour in liquid, adding only enough for creamy consistency (amount will depend on type and moisture content of tofu). Blend until smooth. Turn into prepared crust. Bake 10 minutes. Reduce oven temperature to 350°F and bake until center is firm, about 20 to 25 minutes. Turn off oven and leave cake inside with door ajar for 20 to 30 minutes (this prevents cake from cracking and pulling away from crust). Remove from oven and let cool completely on rack.

Remove cooled cake from pan. Refrigerate until ready to serve.

VARIATIONS:

Top with fresh fruit slices, adding fruit glaze if desired.

Omit lemon juice and peel. Add ¼ cup lightly toasted unsweetened carob powder (see note, p. 64); use grain coffee substitute or decaffeinated coffee for required liquid.

Replace 2 cups tofu with equal amount of mashed avocado. Garnish cake with sliced kiwi and finely chopped pistachios.

Marble Swirl Cheesecake: Blend 2 tablespoons lightly toasted unsweetened carob powder with 1½ cups of cheesecake mixture. Pour in spiral design over tofu mixture in pan. Use knife to swirl through.

Or mix ¼ cup unsweetened cocoa powder, 2 tablespoons natural liquid sweetener, and 1 teaspoon corn oil to form paste. Blend into 1 cup of cheesecake mixture; swirl through mixture in pan.

Add ¼ cup finely crushed toasted almonds to cookie crumb crust. Replace 1 teaspoon vanilla in cheesecake with equal amount of almond extract.

❖ FRESH FRUIT CHARLOTTE ❖

Traditionally, charlottes are made with spongecake or ladyfingers and are filled with a variety of ingredients from fruit to ice cream. In this recipe, decoratively cut slices of whole-grain bread are used with pears and apples.

8 SERVINGS

3	tablespoons margarine
12 to 14	slices whole-grain bread, crusts trimmed and reserved
4	ripe pears, cored and sliced
3	medium-size baking apples, peeled, cored, and sliced
½	teaspoon fresh lemon juice
½	cup unfiltered apple juice
½	cup natural liquid sweetener
2	teaspoons apple pie spice
1	teaspoon ground cinnamon
1	teaspoon vanilla extract
½	cup unsulfured dried currants or raisins

Fruit Glaze (page 85)
Finely chopped toasted almonds or pistachios (optional garnish)
Soy Custard Sauce (see recipe) (optional)

Grease 2-quart charlotte mold or glass baking dish with 1 tablespoon of the margarine. Halve enough of the bread slices to fit around sides of mold. Place side-by-side (not overlapping) around sides of mold. Cut 6 to 8 shapes from remaining bread slices using fancy cutters. Arrange in bottom of mold. Chop all the remaining bread and crusts into small cubes; set aside.

Place pears and apples in large bowl and sprinkle with lemon juice. Add apple juice, sweetener, spices, and vanilla and toss gently until fruit is evenly coated. Fold in currants or raisins.

Preheat oven to 350°F. Spoon one third of fruit mixture into mold; dot with margarine and sprinkle with one third of bread cubes. Repeat two more times, ending with bread cubes. Dot top with remaining margarine. Bake until firm, about 1 hour and 20 minutes. Let cool on rack 10 minutes. Run knife around sides of mold and invert charlotte onto serving plate. Warm fruit glaze over low heat and brush over charlotte. Sprinkle with finely chopped nuts if desired. Serve warm, accompanied with soy custard sauce if you wish.

SOY CUSTARD SAUCE

MAKES ABOUT 2 CUPS

1¾ cups soy milk
¼ cup natural liquid sweetener
1 teaspoon vanilla extract
1 teaspoon grated lemon or orange peel
1½ tablespoons arrowroot

Combine soy milk, sweetener, vanilla, and grated peel in medium-size saucepan. Blend in arrowroot and cook over low heat until thickened. Let sauce cool before serving.

·:· SHARLOTKA WITH ·:· TOFU–ALMOND CREME

6 TO 8 SERVINGS

½ cup (1 stick) margarine
4 cups coarsely crumbled dark pumpernickel bread, crusts removed
5 cups peeled, cored, and thinly sliced Granny Smith apples
1½ teaspoons vanilla extract
1½ cups unsweetened black currant preserves
½ cup Amasake (page 166) or other natural liquid sweetener
1½ teaspoons grated orange peel
2 teaspoons grated lemon peel
½ cup dry red wine or unsweetened red grape juice
½ cup fresh orange juice
⅛ teaspoon ground cloves

Tofu–Almond Creme (see recipe)
Slivered orange and lemon peel (garnish)

Melt 6 tablespoons (¾ stick) margarine in large heavy skillet over medium heat. Add bread crumbs and cook, tossing, until margarine is absorbed. Transfer crumbs to large bowl. Melt remaining 2 tablespoons margarine in small skillet over medium heat. Add apple slices and cook until softened, stirring frequently. Sprinkle vanilla over apples and toss gently. Combine preserves and ¼ cup sweetener in small saucepan and heat through.

Preheat oven to 350°F. Grease 2½-quart baking dish; sprinkle bottom and sides with grated orange and lemon peel. Spread one third of breadcrumbs in bottom of dish. Top with one half of apples and one half of preserves. Repeat with one third of crumbs and remaining apples and preserves. Top with remaining crumbs. Combine wine or grape juice, orange juice, remaining ¼ cup sweetener, and cloves and pour over top. Bake until knife inserted near center comes out clean, about 1½ hours.

Serve warm or at room temperature with Tofu–Almond Creme. Garnish with orange and lemon peel slivers.

TOFU–ALMOND CREME

MAKES ABOUT 2 CUPS

1½ cups tofu
½ cup natural liquid sweetener
3 tablespoons orange flower water (see note)
2 drops almond extract

Combine all ingredients in food processor fitted with steel blade or in blender and blend until smooth. Refrigerate until serving time.

NOTE: *Orange flower water can be purchased in gourmet food and health food stores.*

❖ FRESH FRUIT SHORTCAKE ❖

This is a traditional shortcake, more like a biscuit than a cake. Split apart with a fork, fill with berries or other fresh fruit, and top with soy whip and toasted chopped nuts. The batter can be baked into individual shortcakes or a single 9-inch round.

8 SERVINGS

2 cups whole wheat pastry flour
¼ cup oat flour
2½ teaspoons baking powder
1 teaspoon ground cinnamon
¼ teaspoon salt
½ teaspoon grated orange or lemon peel

½ cup natural liquid sweetener
½ cup corn oil
1½ to 1¾ cups liquid (water, soy milk, or unsweetened fruit juice)
1 teaspoon vanilla extract

FILLING AND TOPPING:
2 cups sliced fresh seasonal fruit (can be marinated in small amount of fruit juice and/or natural liquid sweetener; flavor with grated lemon peel and ground cinnamon if desired)
Creamy Soy Whip (page 173) and/or toasted finely chopped nuts

Preheat oven to 375°F. Grease 9-inch round pan or individual large biscuit rings and baking sheet. Sift together dry ingredients into food processor fitted with steel blade or into large bowl of electric mixer. Stir in orange or lemon peel.

Mix sweetener and oil; add to dry ingredients and blend just until all ingredients are evenly moistened. Combine liquid and vanilla and pour into center of flour mixture all at once. Blend well but do not overbeat (batter will be thick and sticky). Spoon into prepared pan or into rings arranged on greased baking sheet. Bake until lightly browned and crusty, about 20 to 25 minutes, checking after 15 minutes to see that tops are not browning too quickly. Let cool on racks.

To serve, split shortcake with fork as you would an English muffin. Fill with fruit. Garnish with soy whip and /or nuts. *(recipe continues)*

VARIATIONS:

Sprinkle ¾ cup fresh berries with 1 teaspoon arrowroot and toss gently to mix. Stir into batter.

Soak 4 ounces assorted dried fruits in liquid until softened. Drain, using liquid in batter. Chop fruit and stir into batter.

❖ *PINEAPPLE–GINGER* ❖ *UPSIDE-DOWN CAKE*

MAKES ONE 8-INCH SQUARE CAKE

---

 10 tablespoons natural liquid sweetener
 ¾ cup (1½ sticks) margarine
 5 to 7 fresh pineapple slices, each ½ inch thick
 2 heaping tablespoons blackstrap molasses
 5 tablespoons soy milk or grain coffee substitute
 2 cups whole wheat pastry flour
 1 tablespoon ground ginger
 2 teaspoons arrowroot
 1½ teaspoons baking powder
 1 teaspoon ground cinnamon
 ¼ teaspoon ground cloves

Lightly grease sides of 8-inch square pan. Combine 5 tablespoons sweetener and ¼ cup (½ stick) margarine) in small saucepan and place over low heat until margarine is completely melted. Stir well to blend. Pour mixture into prepared pan. Set saucepan aside for later use. Halve pineapple slices if desired; pat dry. Arrange decoratively over syrup mixture in pan.

Combine ½ cup (1 stick) margarine, remaining 5 tablespoons sweetener, and molasses in same saucepan and place over low heat until margarine is completely melted. Stir well to blend. Stir in soy milk or coffee. Remove from heat and let cool.

Preheat oven to 375°F. Sift together dry ingredients into food processor fitted with steel blade or into large bowl of electric mixer. If using processor, pour in molasses mixture and blend briefly using several on/off turns. If using electric mixer, make well in center of dry ingredients and pour in molasses mixture all at once. Blend quickly to moisten dry ingredients; do not overbeat or cake will be dry and heavy. (Batter should pour easily from bowl. If too thick, add small amount of liquid.) Pour batter evenly over pineapple. Bake until top is lightly browned and tester inserted near center comes out clean, about 35 to 40 minutes.

Immediately run knife around edges of pan to loosen cake; invert onto serving plate. Serve warm.

VARIATIONS:

Substitute poached and drained fresh pears or peaches for pineapple.

Cook apple slices in the margarine/sweetener syrup until tender; substitute mixture for pineapple. Cook apples with ¼ cup raisins or dried currants for *French Apple Upside-Down Cake.*

Sprinkle toasted unsweetened coconut and finely chopped toasted pecans or almonds over syrup in bottom of pan before adding fruit, or instead of fruit.

Substitute unsweetened apple juice for soy milk or grain coffee; reduce sweetener slightly.

Coffee Cakes, Yeast Breads, and Quick Breads

BLUEBERRY COFFEE CAKE
CAROB SWIRL COFFEE CAKE
LAST-MINUTE BRUNCH COFFEE CAKE
BASIC SWEET YEAST DOUGH
BLACK WALNUT TEA RING
PHILADELPHIA CINNAMON ROLLS
CHINESE STEAMED DESSERT BUNS
HAMANTASCHEN
APRICOT OR PRUNE QUICK BREAD
SUMMER BERRY BREAD
CRANBERRY–ORANGE BREAD
DATE–NUT BREAD
DECADENT GINGERBREAD WITH APRICOT–RUM SAUCE
ISLAND MACADAMIA–PINEAPPLE BREAD
MOCK MINCEMEAT–MAPLE BREAD
SPICY PUMPKIN–NUT BREAD
ZUCCHINI–PINEAPPLE BREAD

These coffee cakes and sweet breads are a pleasant change from the sweeter dessert-type cakes. Sweet— but not *too* sweet—they are delicious and versatile. Have them by themselves or with yogurt for breakfast, or to liven up a brunch. We Americans don't have a "tea" time, but no matter—these are a perfect mid-afternoon treat!

❖ BLUEBERRY COFFEE CAKE ❖

MAKES ONE 9-INCH SQUARE CAKE

3 cups whole wheat pastry flour
Grated peel of 1 lemon
⅔ cup natural liquid sweetener
¾ cup (1½ sticks) margarine, well chilled and cut into 1-inch pieces

1½ cups water or soy milk
2½ teaspoons baking powder
1 cup blueberries, sorted, rinsed, and drained
½ teaspoon arrowroot

Preheat oven to 350°F. Grease and flour 9-inch square pan. Combine flour and lemon peel in medium-size bowl or food processor fitted with steel blade. Drizzle sweetener over flour mixture and mix briefly to distribute. Add margarine and mix to form uniform crumbs. Reserve ¾ cup mixture for cake topping.

Add water and baking powder to remaining crumb mixture and blend well. Toss blueberries with arrowroot in small bowl; stir into batter. Turn into prepared pan. Sprinkle evenly with topping. Bake until tester inserted in center comes out clean, about 35 to 40 minutes. Serve warm or at room temperature.

❖ CAROB SWIRL COFFEE CAKE ❖

MAKES ONE 8-INCH SQUARE CAKE

3 cups whole wheat pastry flour
⅔ cup natural liquid sweetener
¾ cup (1½ sticks) vegetable or soy margarine, well chilled and cut into 1-inch pieces

1½ cups liquid (water, soy milk, or grain coffee substitute)
2½ teaspoons baking powder
2 tablespoons unsweetened carob powder, lightly toasted (page 64)
2 teaspoons corn oil

Preheat oven to 350°F. Grease and flour 8-inch square pan. Place flour in medium-size bowl or food processor fitted with steel blade. Drizzle in sweetener and mix briefly to distribute. Add margarine and mix to form uniform crumbs. Reserve ¾ cup mixture for cake topping.

Add liquid and baking powder to remaining crumb mixture and blend well. Turn all but ½ cup batter into prepared pan. Mix carob powder and corn oil in cup; blend into reserved ½ cup batter. Drizzle carob mixture over batter in pan and swirl through with knife. Sprinkle evenly with topping. Bake until tester inserted in center comes out clean, about 40 minutes. Serve warm or at room temperature.

❖ LAST-MINUTE BRUNCH COFFEE CAKE ❖

Quick and easy to prepare, this coffee cake is a perfect sweet finale to brunch or afternoon tea.

MAKES ONE 9-INCH SQUARE CAKE

---

     3 cups whole wheat pastry flour
 1½ teaspoons ground cinnamon
     1 teaspoon ground allspice
  ¼ teaspoon freshly grated nutmeg
  ⅔ cup natural liquid sweetener
  ¾ cup (1½ sticks) margarine, well chilled and cut into 1-inch pieces

 1½ cups liquid (water, soy milk, or grain coffee substitute)
 2½ teaspoons baking powder
  ½ cup chopped nuts

Preheat oven to 350°F. Grease and flour 9-inch square pan. Combine flour and spices in medium-size bowl or food processor. Drizzle sweetener over flour mixture and mix briefly to distribute. Add margarine and mix to form uniform crumbs. Reserve ¾ cup mixture for cake topping.

Add liquid and baking powder to remaining crumb mixture and blend well. Stir in nuts. Turn batter into prepared pan. Sprinkle evenly with topping. Bake until tester inserted in center comes out clean, about 35 to 40 minutes. Serve warm or at room temperature.

(recipe continues)

VARIATIONS:

Add ½ cup raisins or dried currants along with nuts.

Substitute ¾ cup mixed fresh lemon and orange juice for half of liquid.

Add 1 teaspoon *each* grated lemon and orange peel.

❖ *BASIC SWEET YEAST DOUGH* ❖

A versatile dough for coffee cakes, rolls, croissants, and other pastries.

---

  1 cup soy milk, warmed to between 105° and 115°F
  1 envelope active dry yeast
  6 tablespoons soy milk
  ¼ cup natural liquid sweetner
  ¼ cup corn oil
  2 tablespoons liquid lecithin
  ½ teaspoon salt (if using oil or unsalted margarine)
3½ cups (or more) whole wheat pastry flour or 3 cups (or
    more) whole wheat pastry flour and ½ cup other
    whole-grain flour (oat, millet, and brown rice are
    especially good)
    Oil for greasing bowl

Pour 1 cup warmed soy milk into medium-size bowl. Sprinkle in yeast, stir to dissolve, and let stand 5 minutes. Stir in 6 tablespoons soy milk, sweetener, corn oil, lecithin, and salt. Add 1½ cups flour and beat well. Transfer dough to a large lightly oiled bowl. Cover with cloth and set in warm, draft-free area (for example, an oven warmed by pilot light) for 40 minutes. Blend in enough additional flour to make workable dough (about 2 cups). Transfer to lightly floured board or pastry cloth and knead ten times. Dough is now ready for rolling and shaping.

VARIATIONS:

Add 1 tablespoon grated lemon or orange peel along with final 2 cups flour.

Add finely chopped dried fruits or nuts along with final 2 cups flour.

Add 1 to 2 teaspoons spices: cinnamon, cardamom, or freshly grated nutmeg.

Sauté a few saffron threads in a small amount of the required oil; let cool completely. Add to yeast mixture. This imparts a delicate yellow, "eggy" color to pastry.

❖ *BLACK WALNUT TEA RING* ❖

MAKES ONE 8- TO 9-INCH RING

---

2 ounces Frangipane Filling (page 90)
¼ cup natural liquid sweetener
1 tablespoon margarine, melted
1 tablespoon unsweetened carob powder, lightly toasted
1 teaspoon vanilla extract
3 ounces (about ¾ cup) chopped black walnuts

Basic Sweet Yeast Dough (page 146)

Soy milk

Blend almond paste, sweetener, margarine, carob, and vanilla in small bowl. Stir in walnuts.

Grease large baking sheet. Roll dough out on lightly floured board or pastry cloth into ¼-inch-thick rectangle about 26 by 10 inches. Spread walnut filling evenly over dough, leaving ½-inch margins. Starting from long edge, roll up to form cylinder and pinch closed. Brush ends of cylinder lightly with water; bring together to form ring and pinch to seal. Transfer to prepared baking sheet. Using floured scissors, cut slits 1½ inches apart around top. If desired, twist dough sections between slits 90 degrees to form decorative wreath. Cover ring with cloth. Set in warm, draft-free area and let rise until doubled in size about 20 to 30 minutes.

Preheat oven to 375°F. Brush top lightly with soy milk. Bake 20 minutes. Brush top again with soy milk and bake until browned, about 10 minutes more. Transfer to rack to cool.   *(recipe continues)*

VARIATIONS:

Add 1 tablespoon grated lemon or orange peel to dough; fill with 1 cup stewed fruit bound with 2 tablespoons cookie or cake crumbs.

Creamy Tofu–Carob Chip Filling: Combine 1½ cups soft tofu, 3 tablespoons natural liquid sweetener, and ½ teaspoon ground cinnamon in food processor fitted with steel blade or blender and blend well. With machine running, slowly pour in 2 tablespoons melted margarine and blend until creamy. Stir in ¼ cup unsweetened carob chips and 3 tablespoons chopped toasted almonds or pistachios if desired.

Apple–Prune Filling: Blend 1 cup unsweetened applesauce, ½ cup chopped cooked prunes, 3 tablespoons crushed cookie crumbs (from shortbread, gingersnaps, or any spice cookie), 2 tablespoons melted margarine, and ½ teaspoon vanilla extract in medium-size bowl. Add 3 tablespoons chopped pecans or walnuts if desired.

Raisins, dried currants, chopped dates, or chopped dried figs can be substituted for prunes.

Lemon–Poppyseed Filling: Combine 3 tablespoons poppyseeds, 3 tablespoons natural liquid sweetener, and 2 tablespoons water or soy milk in small saucepan and bring to boil. Add 1 tablespoon margarine and cook over low heat until margarine is melted. Remove from heat and let cool to lukewarm. Stir in 3 tablespoons Frangipane Filling (page 90), 2 tablespoons cookie or cake crumbs or finely chopped toasted almonds, 1 teaspoon grated lemon peel, and ½ teaspoon fresh lemon juice.

❖ *PHILADELPHIA CINNAMON ROLLS* ❖

These raisin- and nut-studded sweet rolls can be served with break-fast or as dessert. This not-too-sticky version is kinder to both teeth and waistline.

MAKES 1 DOZEN ROLLS

Basic Sweet Yeast Dough (page 146)
1 tablespoon grated lemon peel

½ cup raisins or dried currants
1 teaspoon vanilla extract
¼ cup (½ stick) margarine, at room temperature
¼ cup date sugar or natural liquid sweetener
1½ teaspoons ground cinnamon
½ cup chopped walnuts or pecans

¼ cup natural liquid sweetener (preferably barley malt with corn syrup)

Prepare yeast dough, adding lemon peel.

Combine raisins and vanilla in small bowl. Roll dough out on lightly floured board or pastry cloth into ¼-inch-thick rectangle about 28-by-10 inches. Spread with margarine, leaving ½-inch margins. Sprinkle with ¼ cup date sugar or sweetener, cinnamon, raisin-vanilla mixture, and nuts, distributing evenly. Starting from long edge, roll up to form cylinder and pinch closed.

Generously grease 9-inch square pan. Drizzle remaining ¼ cup sweetener evenly over bottom. Cut dough into twelve slices. Arrange in prepared pan. Cover with cloth. Set in warm, draft-free area until doubled in size, about 40 minutes.

Preheat oven to 350°F. Bake rolls until lightly browned and crusty, about 30 to 40 minutes. Immediately invert onto serving plate. If soft-crusted rolls are desired, transfer to airtight container while still warm.

VARIATIONS:

Replace date sugar or liquid sweetener with equal amount of unsweetened fruit preserves or apple butter.

Replace raisins with ¼ cup unsweetened carob chips.

Substitute any of the fillings for Black Walnut Tea Ring (page 147).

❖ *CHINESE STEAMED DESSERT BUNS* ❖

*An intriguing teatime snack or ending to a Chinese meal. These buns
can be baked rather than steamed if you prefer.*

MAKES ABOUT 2 DOZEN BUNS

YEAST DOUGH:

1 cup water, warmed to between 105° and 115°F
2 tablespoons natural liquid sweetener
1½ teaspoons active dry yeast

3 cups (or more) whole wheat flour *or* 2 cups whole
   wheat flour and 1 cup brown rice flour
1 tablespoon corn oil

TOFU CREME FILLING:

1 cup tofu
¼ cup chopped unsulfured dates, raisins, dried currants,
   dried apricots, or unsweetened carob chips
2 tablespoons natural liquid sweetener
1 tablespoon corn oil
1 tablespoon grain coffee substitute or lightly toasted
   unsweetened carob powder (see note, p. 64)
   (optional)
1 teaspoon liquid lecithin (optional)
1 teaspoon ground cinnamon
2 to 3 tablespoons finely chopped pistachios or toasted
   almonds (optional)
1 tablespoon natural liquid sweetener, mixed with 1
   tablespoon soy milk (if buns are to be baked)

For dough: Combine water and sweetener in small bowl and stir to
blend. Stir in yeast. Let stand until mixture begins to foam, about 10
minutes.

Combine 3 cups flour and oil in large mixing bowl or in food processor
fitted with steel blade. If mixing by hand, make well in center, add yeast
mixture all at once, and stir with fork until dough begins to hold together. If using processor, blend until dough begins to pull away from
sides of work bowl. Transfer dough to lightly floured board or pastry
cloth and knead until smooth, about 5 minutes, adding a little more
flour if dough is too sticky. Shape into ball. Transfer to large oiled bowl,

turning to coat entire surface with oil. Cover with cloth. Let rise in warm, draft-free area until doubled in size, about 45 minutes to 1 hour.

For filling: Combine tofu, dried fruit or carob chips, sweetener, oil, coffee substitute or carob powder, lecithin, and cinnamon in food processor or blender and blend until smooth. Stir in nuts if desired.

To assemble buns: Punch dough down. Roll out into large rectangle ¼ inch thick. Cut into 6-inch squares. Place 2 tablespoons filling on center of each square. Lift up corners toward center, pinch together, and twist to seal. Arrange buns in top tier of Chinese steamer basket (see note). Cover and steam until dough is translucent and fully cooked, about 45 to 50 minutes.

Buns can also be baked. Preheat oven to 375°F. Prick top of each bun once with fork. Brush with sweetener-soy milk mixture. Bake until buns are puffed and lightly browned, about 30 minutes.

VARIATIONS:

Fill buns with ½ recipe of any of the following fillings (or use another of your choice):

Chestnut–Yam Pie filling (page 80)

French Apple–Raisin Tart filling (page 86); substitute pears, peaches, or fresh apricots for apples if desired.

Apple, Pear, and Chestnut Tart filling (page 87); combine chestnut creme with fruit mixture.

NOTE: *Steamer can be purchased at specialty kitchenware stores or Oriental markets. Use according to manufacturer's directions.*

∙:∙ *HAMANTASCHEN* ∙:∙

Prune or poppyseed filling is traditionally used in these holiday pastries. One of the following fillings below uses a combination of dried fruits; the other is a poppyseed filling with a tangy lemon twist.

MAKES ABOUT 56 PASTRIES

FRUIT FILLING:

2 cups mixed unsulfured dried fruit
1¼ cups (more or less) unsweetened fruit juice or water
1 small stick cinnamon
1 teaspoon vanilla extract
¼ teaspoon ground cloves
4 ounces chopped pecans, walnuts, or toasted almonds

POPPYSEED FILLING:

2 tablespoons margarine
1 cup poppyseeds, finely ground
¼ cup raisins or unsulfured dried currants, finely chopped
1 to 2 tablespoons Frangipane Filling (page 90) or nut butter (page 170)
1 teaspoon grated lemon peel
½ teaspoon ground cinnamon

Basic Sweet Yeast Dough (page 146)

1 tablespoon natural liquid sweetener, mixed with 1 tablespoon soy milk and ½ teaspoon ground cinnamon (optional glaze)

For fruit filling: Combine dried fruit and juice or water in medium-size saucepan, using enough liquid to cover fruit. Let fruit soak 1 hour. Add cinnamon stick and simmer over low heat until fruit is tender and no liquid remains, about 30 minutes. Stir in vanilla and cloves. Transfer fruit to food processor fitted with steel blade or blender and puree. Stir in nuts. Let cool completely.

For poppyseed filling: Melt margarine in medium-size saucepan over low heat. Add poppyseeds and cook, stirring, 2 minutes. Stir in remaining ingredients. Remove from heat and let cool completely.

Roll dough out on lightly floured board or pastry cloth into ⅛-inch-thick rectangle about 21-by-28 inches. Cut into 3-inch squares. Place 1 rounded tablespoon filling in center of each square. Pinch corners together over filling, leaving some of filling exposed. Arrange on lightly greased baking sheet. Cover with cloth. Let rise in warm, draft-free area until doubled in size, about 30 to 40 minutes.

Preheat oven to 350°F. Bake until lightly browned, about 40 minutes. If desired, glaze with sweetener-soy milk-cinnamon mixture 10 minutes before end of baking time.

❖ *APRICOT OR PRUNE QUICK BREAD* ❖

MAKES ONE 9-BY-5-INCH LOAF

---

  1 cup unsulfured dried apricots or pitted prunes, snipped
    into small pieces
⅓ cup natural liquid sweetener
⅓ cup fresh orange juice
    Grated peel of 1 lemon or orange

  3 cups whole wheat flour, or 2 cups whole wheat flour
    plus 1 cup whole wheat pastry flour
  1 tablespoon baking powder
1½ cups soy milk
¼ cup corn oil

Preheat oven to 350°F. Grease 9-by-5-inch loaf pan. Combine dried fruit, sweetener, orange juice, and grated peel in medium-size saucepan, place over medium heat, and bring to simmer. Reduce heat and simmer 5 minutes. Let cool.

Combine flour and baking powder; set aside. Mix soy milk and oil in large bowl. Blend in cooled fruit mixture. Add dry ingredients and stir with wooden spoon just until evenly moistened; do not overmix. Turn batter into prepared pan. Bake until tester inserted in center comes out clean, about 50 to 55 minutes. Let cool in pan on rack.

❖ SUMMER BERRY BREAD ❖

This is a great brunch or tea bread; the assorted berries are tempting in appearance and taste.

MAKES ONE 9-BY-5-INCH LOAF

2 cups whole wheat pastry flour
2 teaspoons baking powder
½ teaspoon ground cinnamon
½ cup natural liquid sweetener
5 tablespoons water or soy milk
5 tablespoons corn oil

1 heaping cup assorted fresh berries (raspberries, blackberries, blueberries)
1 tablespoon arrowroot
½ teaspoon grated lemon peel

Preheat oven to 350°F. Grease and flour 9-by-5-inch loaf pan. Place flour, baking powder, and cinnamon in medium-size bowl and stir with fork. Combine sweetener, water or soy milk, and oil in large bowl or food processor fitted with steel blade and blend until creamy. Add dry ingredients all at once and mix until evenly moistened.

Toss berries with arrowroot and grated peel in small bowl; fold into batter. Turn into prepared pan. Bake until tester inserted in center comes out clean, about 40 to 45 minutes. Let cool in pan on rack.

❖ CRANBERRY–ORANGE BREAD ❖

This is an unusual, tangy tea bread that will satisfy a sweet tooth but can also accompany lunch or dinner.

MAKES ONE 9-BY-5-INCH LOAF

1	cup whole wheat flour
1	cup unbleached all-purpose white or whole wheat pastry flour
1½	teaspoons baking powder
½	teaspoon salt (optional)
½	cup natural liquid sweetener
5	tablespoons corn oil
1	cup fresh orange juice
2	teaspoons grated lemon or orange peel
1⅓	cups fresh cranberries
½	cup chopped nuts

Preheat oven to 350°F. Grease 9-by-5-inch loaf pan. Mix dry ingredients in small bowl. Blend sweetener and oil in large bowl or food processor until thickened and creamy. Add juice and peel and blend 1 minute. Add dry ingredients and blend just until evenly mixed. Fold in cranberries and nuts. Turn batter into prepared pan. Bake until tester inserted in center comes out clean, about 1 hour. Let cool in pan on rack.

❖ *DATE–NUT BREAD* ❖

MAKES TWO 9-BY-5-INCH LOAVES

---

  2 cups whole wheat flour
  1 cup unbleached all-purpose white or whole wheat
     pastry flour
2¾ teaspoons baking powder
1½ teaspoons ground cinnamon
  ½ teaspoon salt (optional)
 10 ounces pitted dates, chopped
  5 ounces pecans or walnuts, chopped
  ¾ cup soy milk
  ⅔ cup liquid (fresh orange juice, unfiltered apple juice,
     grain coffee substitute, or decaffeinated coffee)
  ½ cup natural liquid sweetener
  ¼ cup corn or safflower oil

Preheat oven to 350°F. Grease two 9-by-5-inch loaf pans. Stir dry ingredients together with fork in medium-size bowl. Transfer 1 teaspoon of mixture to small bowl, add dates and nuts, and toss to coat. Combine soy milk, liquid, sweetener, and oil in large bowl or food processor fitted with steel blade and blend until thickened. Add dry ingredients and blend just until evenly mixed. Fold in dates and nuts. Divide batter between prepared pans. Bake until tester inserted in center comes out clean, about 65 minutes.

Let breads cool in pans on rack. When cooled, wrap in plastic or waxed paper. Store in airtight container overnight before serving.

VARIATIONS:

Substitute 5 ounces chopped dried apricots or cherries for half of dates.

❖ DECADENT GINGERBREAD WITH ❖ APRICOT–RUM SAUCE

This spicy bread is rich and moist, with blackstrap molasses and grain coffee substitute adding to its flavor and texture. Bake a day or two ahead for best results.

MAKES TWO 9-BY-5-INCH LOAVES

¾ cup natural liquid sweetener
½ cup blackstrap molasses
5 tablespoons corn oil
2¾ cups whole wheat pastry flour
1 tablespoon ground ginger
2 teaspoons baking powder
1 teaspoon ground cinnamon
1 teaspoon ground allspice
1 teaspoon grated lemon or orange peel (optional)
½ teaspoon salt (optional)
1½ cups grain coffee substitute or decaffeinated coffee, heated

Apricot-Rum Sauce (see recipe)

Preheat oven to 350°F. Grease and flour two 9-by-5-inch loaf pans. Combine sweetener, molasses, and oil in large bowl or food processor and blend well. Combine dry ingredients in separate bowl and stir with fork. Add dry ingredients to molasses mixture alternately with hot liquid, beginning and ending with dry ingredients (batter should be pourable; if too thick, add a bit more hot liquid). Divide batter between prepared pans. Bake until tester inserted in center comes out clean, about 60 to 70 minutes. Let breads cool in pans on rack until lukewarm; wrap in waxed paper, then plastic. Let stand in cool area at least overnight or up to 3 days before serving.

VARIATIONS:
Apple Gingerbread: Peel and core 1 large cooking apple; cut into thin slices. Dredge slices in small amount of flour and cinnamon. Overlap slices atop batter in pans. Bake as directed.

Filled Gingerbread Cupcakes: Grease muffin tins or line with paper muffin cups. Fill half full with batter. Add one level to heaping tablespoon
(recipe continues)

Spicy Applesauce with Raisins (page 167), or Creamy Tofu Cheese Filling (page 175) to each. Top with batter, filling cups two thirds full. Bake until tops of cupcakes spring back when pressed lightly with finger (time will vary according to size of muffin tins).

Gingerbread Fruitcake: Chop ½ to ¾ cup assorted dried fruits into small pieces; dredge in small amount of flour and cinnamon. Fold into batter and bake as directed.

APRICOT–RUM SAUCE

MAKES ABOUT 2 CUPS

1½ cups fresh apricots peeled, pitted and chopped, or use canned apricots, drained
½ cup water
1 teaspoon grated orange or lemon peel
½ cup chopped nuts
1 teaspoon natural alcohol-free rum flavoring

Puree apricots in a blender or food processor fitted with a steel blade. Combine apricot puree, water, and grated peel in small heavy saucepan and bring to boil. Simmer 5 minutes, stirring constantly. Remove from heat and stir in nuts and rum flavoring. Serve warm over gingerbread slices.

VARIATION:
Substitute peaches for apricots.

❖ ISLAND MACADAMIA–PINEAPPLE BREAD ❖

MAKES ONE 9-BY-5-INCH LOAF

2¼ cups whole wheat pastry flour
2½ teaspoons baking powder
½ teaspoon salt (optional)
½ cup natural liquid sweetener
3 tablespoons corn oil
1½ cups fresh or canned unsweetened crushed pineapple
¾ cup fresh orange juice or coconut milk
1 teaspoon vanilla extract
½ cup unsweetened grated coconut
9 ounces macadamia nuts

Preheat oven to 350°F. Grease 9-by-5-inch loaf pan. Combine dry ingredients in medium-size bowl and stir with fork. Blend sweetener and oil in large bowl or food processor fitted with steel blade until creamy. Mix pineapple, juice or coconut milk, and vanilla in separate bowl. Add dry ingredients to creamed mixture alternately with pineapple, beginning and ending with dry ingredients. Fold in coconut and nuts. Turn batter into prepared pan. Bake until tester inserted in center comes out clean, about 60 to 70 minutes. Let cool in pan on rack.

❖ *MOCK MINCEMEAT–MAPLE BREAD* ❖

A holiday favorite.

MAKES ONE 9-BY-5-INCH LOAF

---

    2 cups whole wheat pastry flour
 1½ teaspoons baking powder
  ½ cup corn oil
  ½ cup maple syrup
  ½ cup grain coffee substitute or decaffeinated coffee
  ½ teaspoon natural alcohol-free rum flavoring (optional)
1¾ cups Dried Fruit Filling (page 169)
  ¼ cup chopped nuts (optional)

Preheat oven to 350°F. Grease 9-by-5-inch loaf pan. Combine flour and baking powder in large bowl or food processor fitted with steel blade. Mix oil, syrup, coffee, and rum flavoring and add to dry ingredients. Add mock mincemeat and blend well. Turn batter into prepared pan. Sprinkle with nuts if desired. Bake until tester inserted in center comes out clean, about 50 to 60 minutes. Let cool in pan on rack.

❖ *SPICY PUMPKIN–NUT BREAD* ❖

MAKES ONE 9-BY-5-INCH LOAF

---

2 cups whole wheat pastry flour
2 teaspoons baking powder
1 teaspoon pumpkin pie spice
½ teaspoon ground cinnamon
½ teaspoon ground ginger
1 cup pureed fresh-cooked or canned pumpkin
½ cup corn oil
5 tablespoons natural liquid sweetener
¼ cup liquid (water, unfiltered apple juice, or grain coffee
  substitute)
1 teaspoon vanilla extract
½ cup chopped pecans
½ cup raisins (optional)

Preheat oven to 350°F. Grease 9-by-5-inch loaf pan. Place flour, baking powder, and spices in medium-size bowl and stir with fork. Combine pumpkin, oil, sweetener, liquid, and vanilla in large bowl or food processor and blend well. Add dry ingredients and mix only until evenly moistened. Fold in pecans and raisins if desired. Turn batter into prepared pan. Bake until tester inserted in center comes out clean, about 60 to 70 minutes. Let cool in pan on rack.

❖ *ZUCCHINI–PINEAPPLE BREAD* ❖

This bread is wonderfully moist. No one will guess that it's made with zucchini!

MAKES ONE 9-BY-5-INCH LOAF

2¼ cups whole wheat pastry flour
2 teaspoons baking powder
½ teaspoon salt (optional)
½ teaspoon ground cinnamon
¼ teaspoon freshly grated nutmeg
½ cup corn oil
½ cup unsweetened pineapple juice or water
5 tablespoons natural liquid sweetener
1 teaspoon vanilla extract
¾ cup crushed fresh or canned unsweetened pineapple
1½ cups grated zucchini
½ teaspoon grated lemon peel (optional)

Preheat oven to 350°F. Grease and flour 9-by-5-inch loaf pan. Combine dry ingredients in medium-size bowl and stir with fork. Blend oil, juice or water, sweetener, and vanilla in large bowl or food processor fitted with a steel blade until creamy. Add flour mixture alternately with pineapple, beginning and ending with dry ingredients. Stir in zucchini and grated peel. Turn batter into prepared pan. Bake until tester inserted in center comes out clean, about 60 to 65 minutes. Let cool in pan on rack. Wrap in plastic and let stand overnight before serving.

VARIATIONS:

Add ½ cup chopped nuts or raisins to batter.

Substitute grated carrot for zucchini. Add ¼ teaspoon ground cloves to dry ingredients.

Fillings, Frostings, Glazes, and Sauces

AMASAKE

SPICY APPLESAUCE WITH RAISINS

APPLE BUTTER

COCONUT–PECAN FILLING AND TOPPING

FLAXSEED WHIP

DRIED FRUIT FILLING

QUICK MAPLE FROSTING

NUT BUTTERS

OAT CREME

RICE CREME

VANILLA SOY CAKE FROSTING

SOY SOUR CREAM

CREAMY SOY WHIP

STREUSEL TOPPING

CREAMY TOFU CHEESE FILLING

TOFU WHIP

APPLE CIDER GLAZE

CITRUS GLAZE

CRANBERRY–ORANGE GLAZE

FRESH FRUIT DESSERT TOPPING

QUICK FRUIT SAUCE

MAPLE GLAZE

PIÑA COLADA DESSERT SAUCE

RED BEAN DESSERT SAUCE

FILLINGS AND FROSTINGS

There is something absolutely irresistible about a luscious look-ing frosting or filling. Many a pristine frosting job has been ruined when someone couldn't help taking "just a taste," leaving those telltale finger marks! Here are a few fillings and frostings, in ad-dition to those already included in various recipes throughout the book. When the creative sweet tooth strikes, try mix-and-matching your favorite combinations.

❖ *AMASAKE* ❖

Amasake has many uses in dessert making. In its thickened state it can be used as a filling like rice or oat creme. Thinner amasake can be cooked down into a glaze, or refrigerated and served as a refreshing drink.

---

3 cups sweet brown rice
6 cups water
⅓ cup koji (fermented rice bacteria, which turn rice starch into sugar)

Wash rice twice under running water; drain. Combine with 6 cups water in large saucepan and let soak overnight.

The next day, bring to boil over high heat, then reduce heat and simmer 25 minutes. Remove from heat; let stand at room temperature 1 hour. Mix in koji. Transfer mixture to large glass bowl. Cover with cloth. Place bowl in warm draft-free area such as oven warmed by pilot light. Allow to ferment 6 to 8 hours, stirring occasionally to make sure koji is evenly distributed (the longer the fermentation, the sweeter the amasake will be).

Drain sweet liquid from bowl into saucepan. Boil until liquid darkens and thickens slightly. Let cool and refrigerate. Serve as a beverage or use as a sweet syrup to flavor other drinks.

Rice mixture remaining in bowl can be cooked until lightly browned, then pureed in blender or food processor until smooth. Use as a creme filling or binder in desserts or cooking, flavoring as desired.

❖ *SPICY APPLESAUCE WITH RAISINS* ❖

Serve on its own as dessert, or use as a filling for cake layers, pies, cupcakes, or pastry. There are no set quantities for the ingredients— just flavor to taste. Allow 2 apples per serving if applesauce is to be served as dessert.

Cooking apples, peeled and cored
Unsweetened fruit juice or water
Natural liquid sweetener (optional)
Unsulfured raisins or currants, soaked and drained
(optional)
Ground cinnamon, ground cloves, and freshly grated nutmeg
to taste
Grated lemon peel (optional)

Place apples in heavy skillet or saucepan with tight-fitting lid. Add just enough liquid to cover bottom of pan. Cover and steam over medium-low heat until apples are soft. Transfer apples to blender, food processor, or food mill and puree. Sweeten if desired; add raisins or currants, spices, and lemon peel. Refrigerate until serving time.

❖ *APPLE BUTTER* ❖

Use as a spread, to fill individual tartlets, or between cake layers.

MAKES ABOUT 2½ QUARTS

6 pounds tart apples, cored and peeled
6 cups unfiltered apple juice or cider
  Natural liquid sweetener to taste
2 teaspoons ground cinnamon
½ teaspoon ground cloves

Combine apples and juice in large kettle or Dutch oven and simmer until apples are soft, about 30 minutes. Drain. Puree apples in food mill or food processor. Blend in sweetener and spices. Transfer to airtight container and refrigerate.

❖ *COCONUT–PECAN FILLING* ❖
AND TOPPING

Spread this between and on top of carob or chocolate cake–it's a less sweet and dairy-free version of the traditional German Chocolate Cake filling.

MAKES ENOUGH FOR ONE 8- OR 9-INCH CAKE

1½ cups soy milk
2 tablespoons natural liquid sweetener
2 teaspoons arrowroot, dissolved in small amount of water
¼ cup flaked or shredded unsweetened coconut
¼ cup chopped pecans
1½ teaspoons vanilla extract

Combine soy milk and sweetener in medium-size saucepan. Stir in arrowroot mixture. Place over medium heat and stir until mixture begins to thicken. Remove from heat and blend in coconut, pecans, and vanilla. Spread over cake layers while filling is still warm, or let cool and refrigerate in covered container. If filling becomes too thick on chilling, rewarm over low heat and thin with a bit more soy milk.

❖ *FLAXSEED WHIP* ❖

This topping is similar in texture to whipped egg whites. It can be folded into mousses or spooned on top of pies as a meringue substitute. Unlike egg white toppings, though, this cannot be baked or heated.

MAKES ABOUT 2 CUPS

---

3 cups cold water
5 tablespoons flaxseed

1 tablespoon maple syrup (optional)

Combine water and flaxseed in large saucepan and soak for 1 hour.

Simmer mixture for 20 minutes, then remove from heat. Let cool. Pour through strainer set over bowl (seeds can be reserved and added to bread or muffin batter if desired). Refrigerate liquid until well chilled.

Beat chilled liquid with egg beater or electric mixer until fluffy. Spoon whip over pies, tarts, or puddings. Drizzle with maple syrup if desired.

❖ DRIED FRUIT FILLING ❖

MAKES ABOUT 3 CUPS

---

  3 cups mixed dried fruits (apples, apricots, figs, peaches, pears, prunes, raisins)
1¼ cups fresh orange juice
  1 cup water
  1 stick cinnamon
  2 whole cloves
  ½ cup slivered blanched almonds

Combine fruits, orange juice, and water in large nonaluminum saucepan and let soak about 1 hour. Add spices and soak 1 to 2 hours longer. Place over medium heat and cook until fruit is tender, about 20 minutes. Drain off any excess liquid; discard whole spices. Stir almonds into fruit mixture.

❖ QUICK MAPLE FROSTING ❖

MAKES ABOUT 2 CUPS (FOR TWO 9-INCH LAYERS)

1½ cups soy milk powder
  ½ cup natural liquid sweetener
  5 tablespoons fresh orange juice
  2 teaspoons vanilla extract

Whirl all ingredients in blender or use a wire whisk to blend to a creamy consistency. *(recipe continues)*

VARIATIONS:

Lemon Frosting: Substitute 3 tablespoons fresh lemon juice for equal amount of orange juice. Add ½ teaspoon finely grated lemon peel.

Orange Frosting: Add ½ teaspoon finely grated orange peel.

Mocha Frosting: Add 2 tablespoons lightly toasted unsweetened carob powder and grain coffee substitute for orange juice.

•⁙• *NUT BUTTERS* •⁙•

Nut butters are good binders and can be used in pies, tarts, or to fill a layer cake. A small amount of nut butter spread over the bottom of a baked pie or tart crust before filling will keep the crust from becoming soggy. Remember that, while rich in nutrients, nut butters are also high in calories.

MAKES ABOUT 1 CUP

1¼ cups crushed nuts (pecans, walnuts, blanched almonds, cashews, or peanuts)
½ cup (1 stick) margarine
Optional flavorings: fruit puree; ground cinnamon; almond extract; vanilla extract; unsweetened carob powder, or powdered grain coffee substitute

---

Combine nuts and margarine in blender or food processor and blend at high speed until creamy. If necessary, add a few drops liquid. Flavor as desired. Transfer to airtight container and refrigerate.

❖ OAT CREME ❖

MAKES ABOUT 3 CUPS

1½ cups rolled oats
 4 cups liquid (water, unsweetened fruit juice, or soy
   milk)
3 to 5 tablespoons natural liquid sweetener
 2 teaspoons nut butter
 1 1-inch piece vanilla bean, split open, or 1 teaspoon
   vanilla extract
 1 teaspoon ground cinnamon
 ¼ teaspoon freshly grated nutmeg (optional)

Toast oats in large heavy skillet over medium heat until lightly browned, stirring frequently. Add remaining ingredients and bring mixture to rolling boil over high heat. Reduce heat and simmer until thickened, about 15 to 20 minutes, adding liquid if mixture becomes too thick. Let cool. Transfer to airtight container and refrigerate.

❖ RICE CREME ❖

Great as a pie or tart filling or as a binder in cakes and sauces.

MAKES ABOUT 3 CUPS

---

2 cups cooked sweet or plain brown rice (see note)
1 cup (or more) liquid (water, unsweetened fruit juice, soy
  milk, grain coffee substitute, or decaffeinated coffee)
  Natural liquid sweetener to taste (optional)
  Optional flavorings: grated lemon or orange peel; ground
  cinnamon, allspice, or freshly grated nutmeg; natural
  flavoring extract; finely chopped nuts; pureed or chopped
  fruits; toasted coconut

Combine rice and liquid in blender or food processor and blend until smooth and creamy. Add flavorings, nuts, or fruit, adjusting consistency with more liquid if necessary.   *(recipe continues)*

NOTE: *Sweet brown rice (available at natural foods stores) is best for rice creme, since it is more glutinous than regular brown rice. To cook sweet brown rice, use 2 cups liquid to 1 cup raw rice.*

❖ VANILLA SOY CAKE FROSTING ❖

MAKES ENOUGH TO FILL AND FROST 9-INCH LAYER CAKE

1½ cups soy milk powder
½ cup unsweetened fruit juice
5 tablespoons maple syrup or other light natural liquid
   sweetener
2 teaspoons vanilla extract

Combine all ingredients in blender or food processor and blend at high speed until creamy and smooth. Use as soon as possible (if frosting begins to separate, blend again briefly until thickened), by spreading between cake layers or on cupcakes. Frosting can also be piped through pastry bag for garnish. Store in refrigerator.

VARIATION:

For a *carob frosting*, add 2 tablespoons lightly toasted carob powder (page 64) to rest of ingredients and proceed with recipe.

❖ SOY SOUR CREAM ❖

Can be used as a topping for cakes or pies or in a variety of creamy fillings. Tightly covered, this will keep for at least 2 weeks in the refrigerator.

MAKES ABOUT 1¾ cups

10 ounces soft tofu
½ cup liquid lecithin or vegetable oil
2 to 4 tablespoons (or to taste) fresh lemon juice
4 teaspoons natural liquid sweetener (optional)

Combine all ingredients in blender or food processor and blend until smooth and creamy. Cover and refrigerate; mixture will thicken slightly on chilling.

•:• *CREAMY SOY WHIP* •:•

Lighter in texture than Tofu Whip (page 175), this can be used as a topping or folded into other fillings to make a mousse. For special occasions, pipe through a pastry bag to form rosettes and other decorations.

MAKES ABOUT 1½ CUPS

½ cup soy milk, well chilled
1 cup vegetable oil
1½ tablespoons maple syrup
1 teaspoon vanilla extract *or* seeds from ½-inch piece vanilla bean
Pinch of salt

Combine soy milk and ½ cup oil in blender and blend at medium speed. With machine running, slowly pour in remaining oil; mixture will thicken. Add remaining ingredients and blend a few seconds longer. Use as soon as possible (if whip begins to separate, blend again briefly until thickened). Store in refrigerator.

VARIATIONS:

Add 1 to 2 tablespoons lightly toasted carob powder (page 64).

Add ¼ teaspoon ground cinnamon.

Add ½ teaspoon powdered grain coffee substitute.

Add ¼ teaspoon of any pure alcohol-free flavoring of your choice, such as mint, rum, brandy, almond, vanilla etc.

Add ½ teaspoon finely grated orange or lemon peel.

Add 3 tablespoons finely chopped dried fruits. To soften, soak them in water until soft, about 1½ hours, drain, then squeeze in a towel to remove excess water, if necessary. *(recipe continues)*

Add any of the following colorings (see also page 18):
½ teaspoon pure unsweetened cherry juice.
½ teaspoon pure chlorophyll juice.
Add ¼ teaspoon ground ginger.

NOTE: *Pure unsweetened cherry juice and liquid chlorophyll can be purchased in health food stores*

∴ *STREUSEL TOPPING* ∴

A basic crumbly topping for sprinkling on coffee cakes and pies.

MAKES ENOUGH FOR ONE 8- OR 9-INCH CAKE OR PIE

---

   1 cup whole wheat pastry flour
1½ teaspoons ground cinnamon
   ¾ cup (1½ sticks) margarine
   ½ cup natural liquid sweetener

Combine flour and cinnamon in bowl or food processor. Add margarine and mix until crumbly. Drizzle sweetener evenly over mixture and toss with fork (in processor, blend using on/off turns) until well mixed. Sprinkle streusel over coffee cake or pie and bake as directed in recipe.

VARIATIONS:

Add 1 heaping tablespoon lightly toasted unsweetened carob powder (see note, p. 64).

Add grated lemon or orange peel to taste.

❖ CREAMY TOFU CHEESE FILLING ❖

Similar to cream cheese, this filling can be flavored as you like and used in tarts, pies, cupcakes, or for a quick cheesecake.

MAKES ABOUT 2¼ CUPS

2 cups soft tofu
3 tablespoons fresh lemon juice
3 tablespoons vegetable oil
2 tablespoons natural liquid sweetener (optional)
Water or soy milk

Combine tofu, lemon juice, oil, and sweetener in blender or food processor and blend until smooth, adding just enough water for creamy consistency. Cover and refrigerate (mixture will thicken slightly on chilling).

❖ TOFU WHIP ❖

This can be flavored however you like; try adding chopped dried fruit (soaked if necessary), flavoring extracts, or spices.

MAKES ABOUT 1½ CUPS

1⅓ cups firm tofu
3 tablespoons maple syrup
2 tablespoons almond or cashew butter
½ teaspoon vanilla extract

Combine all ingredients in blender and blend at medium speed until creamy and smooth. Refrigerate until ready to use.

GLAZES AND SAUCES

Glazes and sauces enhance the flavor as well as the visual appeal of a dessert. A glaze is usually lighter and lower in calories than a frosting, but adds just enough decorative finish. Many of the glazes below require little if any sweetener, being simply thickened unsweetened fruit juice. The sauces are richer than the glazes but still keep the calories to a minimum. Spoon over your favorite crepe, pastry, soy ice cream, or leftover cake.

❖ APPLE CIDER GLAZE ❖

Great for a shiny finish to tea breads and pie fillings. Other fruit juices can be substituted for apple cider; add a small amount of soy milk for a creamy-looking glaze.

MAKES ABOUT 2 CUPS

½ cup water
1 tablespoon arrowroot
1½ cups unfiltered apple cider
1 teaspoon ground cinnamon

Combine water and arrowroot in small bowl; set aside. Mix cider and cinnamon in small heavy saucepan and bring to boil over high heat. Reduce heat, add arrowroot mixture, and cook, whisking until glaze is thickened and reduced by about half. Remove from heat. Serve warm, or let cool and store in refrigerator.

❖ CITRUS GLAZE ❖

Use to glaze rolls, pies or tarts, and cakes.

MAKES ABOUT 1 CUP

1 tablespoon arrowroot
1¼ cups water
¾ cup fresh or reconstituted frozen unsweetened orange
   juice
1 tablespoon fresh lemon or lime juice
½ teaspoon finely grated lemon peel

Combine arrowroot with small amount of water in small saucepan to form thin paste. Add remaining water and orange juice and blend well. Bring to boil; cook over medium heat 1 minute, stirring constantly. Remove from heat. Stir in lemon juice and grated peel. Use while warm.

❖ *CRANBERRY–ORANGE GLAZE* ❖

MAKES ABOUT 1½ CUPS

---

  1 cup cranberry juice
  ½ cup fresh orange juice
    Natural liquid sweetener to taste
1½ tablespoons arrowroot
  1 teaspoon finely grated orange peel (optional)

Combine all ingredients in blender and mix well. Pour into small heavy saucepan and bring to boil, whisking constantly. Stir over low heat until mixture thickens. Let cool slightly. Brush glaze over pie, tart, or pastry.

❖ *FRESH FRUIT DESSERT TOPPING* ❖

Serve warm or chilled over puddings, soy ice creme, or cake.

MAKES ABOUT 4 CUPS

1½ cups unfiltered apple juice
  ¼ cup (or less) natural liquid sweetener (depending on
    sweetness of fruit)
  4 peaches, peeled, pitted, and sliced ¼ inch thick
  2 bananas, peeled, sliced, and sprinkled with fresh lemon
    juice
  1 cup pitted Bing cherries

Combine juice and sweetener in medium-size saucepan and bring to boil. Reduce heat and simmer until mixture is reduced by one third, stirring occasionally. Stir in fruit and simmer 5 more minutes.

❖ QUICK FRUIT SAUCE ❖

Chopped or mashed fresh fruit
Natural liquid sweetener to taste
Natural flavoring extract to taste (optional)

Combine fruit and sweetener in heavy saucepan and cook over low heat until thickened and reduced. Remove from heat and stir in extract if desired. Serve warm or cooled.

❖ MAPLE GLAZE ❖

A basic quick glaze that can be flavored as you wish—try unsweetened carob, cocoa, or grain coffee substitute, natural flavoring extracts, or ground cinnamon.

6 SERVINGS

1 cup maple syrup

Place syrup in small heavy saucepan and bring to boil. Remove from heat and let cool slightly. Spoon or brush over dessert.

VARIATION:

Lemon-Maple Glaze: Add two tablespoons fresh lemon juice to syrup.

❖ PIÑA COLADA DESSERT SAUCE ❖

Using Amasake (page 166) for the sweetener adds a slightly liqueur-like taste. If at all possible, use fresh coconut milk and shredded fresh coconut instead of soy milk and packaged coconut. This sauce is spectacular served over pineapple-filled crepes.

MAKES ABOUT 2¾ CUPS

1½ cups fresh coconut milk or soy milk
¼ cup natural liquid sweetener
1 tablespoon arrowroot, dissolved in small amount of
   water
3 ounces freshly grated or unsweetened packaged coconut
1 teaspoon vanilla extract

Combine coconut milk or soy milk and sweetener in medium-size heavy saucepan and warm over medium heat. Whisk in arrowroot mixture and cook until sauce is thickened and clear, about 10 minutes, stirring. Remove from heat and stir in coconut and vanilla. Let cool, then cover and refrigerate.

❖ RED BEAN DESSERT SAUCE ❖

Don't be put off by the unusual-sounding name. It's delicious spooned over Real Vanilla Bean Ice Creme (page 210), rice pudding, or custard. Sauce will keep 2 to 3 days in refrigerator.

MAKES 2½ TO 3 CUPS

---

1 cup azuki beans (available in natural foods stores and Oriental markets)
2 cups water
1 3-inch stick cinnamon
½ cup natural liquid sweetener
1 teaspoon vanilla extract
  Water or unsweetened fruit juice (optional)

Rinse beans. Soak in water to cover overnight.

Drain beans; rinse again. Place beans and 2 cups water in medium-size heavy saucepan along with cinnamon stick. Bring to boil, then reduce heat and cook until beans are tender, 30 to 40 minutes.

Remove from heat; discard cinnamon stick. Let beans cool to lukewarm. Transfer to blender along with sweetener and vanilla and blend until smooth. Thin with small amount of additional water or fruit juice if desired.

Puddings

FRENCH CARAMELIZED APPLE PUDDING
OLD FASHIONED WHOLE WHEAT BREAD PUDDING
CARROT RAISIN PUDDING
CITRUS SNOW PUDDING
STEAMED FIG PUDDING
INDIAN PUDDING
PUMPKIN PUDDING
SWEET POTATO PUDDING
TAPIOCA WITH FRESH FRUIT
TWO-TONE CRUMB PARFAIT

Puddings are especially warming and comforting desserts. Made with healthful ingredients as these are, they provide plenty of nutritional value, too.

❖ FRENCH CARAMELIZED ❖ APPLE PUDDING

6 SERVINGS

6 large baking apples, peeled, cored, and cut into ½-inch-thick slices
1 cup dry white wine or Amasake (page 166)
¾ cup natural liquid sweetener
1 teaspoon ground ginger
¼ teaspoon freshly grated nutmeg
3 whole cloves

Preheat oven to 350°F. Grease 9-inch round or square baking dish. Combine apple slices and wine or amasake in large bowl and toss to coat. Pour ¼ cup sweetener into prepared baking dish. Sprinkle evenly with spices. Arrange apple slices in dish and drizzle remaining sweetener over. Bake until apples are very tender, about 1 hour, basting several times with juices. Serve warm.

❖ OLD FASHIONED WHOLE WHEAT ❖ BREAD PUDDING

Leftover dry cake cubes can be substituted for bread. To dry either bread or cake, leave slices unwrapped for a day or place in 200°F oven for 30 minutes, then cut into cubes.

6 TO 8 SERVINGS

4 cups dry whole wheat bread cubes
2 cups soy milk, warmed
½ cup natural liquid sweetener
½ cup raisins
¼ cup (½ stick) margarine, melted
¼ cup unfiltered apple juice
¼ cup chopped nuts
1½ tablespoons arrowroot
1 teaspoon ground cinnamon

Preheat oven to 350°F. Grease 2-quart baking dish. Place bread cubes in large bowl. Pour warmed soy milk over and toss to coat. Combine all remaining ingredients and stir into bread mixture. Turn into prepared baking dish. Bake until knife inserted in center comes out clean, about 40 minutes. Serve warm or at room temperature.

❖ *CARROT–RAISIN PUDDING* ❖

6 SERVINGS

---

    1 cup grated carrot
    ¾ cup raisins
    ½ cup natural liquid sweetener
    5 tablespoons corn oil
    3 tablespoons unfiltered apple juice
 1¼ cups whole wheat pastry flour
 1½ teaspoons baking powder
    ½ teaspoon ground cinnamon
    ¼ teaspoon freshly grated nutmeg

Preheat oven to 350°F. Grease 1-quart baking dish or six individual custard cups. Combine carrot, raisins, sweetener, oil, and apple juice in mixing bowl. Sift together dry ingredients and add to carrot mixture. Stir just until evenly moistened; do not overmix. Turn mixture into prepared baking dish or cups. Bake until knife inserted in center comes out clean, about 1 to 1¼ hours for baking dish (less for individual cups). Serve warm or at room temperature.

•:• *CITRUS SNOW PUDDING* •:•

This frothy pudding is traditionally made with whipped egg whites.
This recipe substitutes flaxseed whip to make a dairy-free version.

4 TO 6 SERVINGS

---

2 cups water
⅔ cup natural liquid sweetener
¼ cup fresh lemon, orange, or lime juice
2 tablespoons agar-agar flakes

1 cup Flaxseed Whip (page 168)
  Mint sprigs or thin lemon, orange, or lime slices
  (garnish)

Bring water to boil in medium-size saucepan over high heat. Stir in sweetener, juice, and agar-agar and return to boil. Reduce heat and simmer until flakes are completely dissolved. Remove from heat and let cool completely.

Fold in flaxseed whip. Spoon mixture into goblets or parfait glasses. Chill until serving time. Garnish with mint or fruit slices.

•:• *STEAMED FIG PUDDING* •:•

6 SERVINGS

¾ cup soy milk
½ cup natural liquid sweetener
3 tablespoons vegetable or soy margarine
1½ cups whole wheat pastry flour
½ teaspoon baking powder
½ teaspoon ground cinnamon
½ teaspoon ground allspice
⅛ teaspoon ground cloves
8 ounces unsulfered dried figs, chopped

Preheat oven to 350°F. Generously grease 1½-quart baking dish. Combine soy milk, sweetener, and margarine in small saucepan and place over low heat just until margarine is melted. Let cool slightly. Sift dry ingredients into large bowl. Add margarine mixture and stir just until evenly moistened; do not overmix. Stir in figs. Turn mixture into prepared baking dish. Cover with waxed paper, then with tightly fitting lid or sheet of aluminum foil.

Set rack into large roasting pan. Place pudding on rack. Add enough simmering water to roasting pan to come one third up sides of baking dish. Bake until knife inserted in center of pudding comes out clean, about 2 hours. Serve warm or at room temperature.

❖ *INDIAN PUDDING* ❖

4 TO 6 SERVINGS

3¾ cups soy milk
¼ cup yellow cornmeal

½ cup natural liquid sweetener
½ cup raisins
¼ cup corn oil
1 teaspoon vanilla extract
1 teaspoon ground cinnamon
1 teaspoon ground ginger
½ teaspoon salt

Grease 1½-quart baking dish; set aside. Pour 2 cups soy milk into double-boiler top and place over simmering water until heated through. Combine ¼ cup cold soy milk with cornmeal. Stir into hot soy milk. Cook over simmering water 20 minutes, stirring frequently.

Preheat oven to 250°F. Stir sweetener, raisins, oil, vanilla, spices, and salt into cornmeal mixture. Turn into prepared baking dish. Pour remaining 1½ cups soy milk over. Bake 3 hours. Let cool 30 minutes before serving.

❖ *PUMPKIN PUDDING* ❖

4 TO 6 SERVINGS

1½ cups soy milk
1 cup fresh-cooked or canned pumpkin
½ cup whole wheat pastry flour
2 teaspoons vanilla extract
½ teaspoon ground cinnamon
¼ teaspoon salt
⅛ teaspoon ground cloves
⅛ teaspoon freshly grated nutmeg

Preheat oven to 350°F. Grease 1-quart baking dish. Combine all ingredients in mixing bowl and blend well. Turn into prepared dish. Bake until knife inserted in center comes out clean, about 40 minutes. Serve warm or at room temperature.

❖ *SWEET POTATO PUDDING* ❖

This is a rich pudding that can be served as dessert or as a side dish; in the latter case, reduce sweetener to 3 tablespoons and omit raisins and nuts.

6 SERVINGS

---

4 cups grated sweet potato
2 cups soy milk
⅔ cup natural liquid sweetener
½ cup raisins or unsulfured dried currants
¼ cup (½ stick) vegetable or soy margarine, melted
1½ tablespoons arrowroot
1 teaspoon ground cinnamon
½ teaspoon ground ginger
¼ teaspoon ground cloves
¼ teaspoon freshly grated nutmeg
½ cup chopped pecans

Preheat oven to 350°F. Grease 2-quart baking dish. Combine all ingredients except pecans and blend well. Turn mixture into prepared baking dish. Sprinkle with nuts. Bake until knife inserted in center comes out clean, about 45 minutes. Serve warm or at room temperature.

•:• *TAPIOCA WITH FRESH FRUIT* •:•

6 TO 8 SERVINGS

3 cups sliced assorted fresh fruits
9 tablespoons natural liquid sweetener
1 teaspoon ground cinnamon
2 cups boiling water
⅓ cup tapioca
¼ teaspoon salt

Preheat oven to 350°F. Grease 2-quart baking dish. Arrange fruit in prepared dish. Mix 4 tablespoons sweetener and cinnamon and drizzle over fruit. Bake for 15 minutes.

Meanwhile, combine all remaining ingredients in medium-size saucepan and cook over medium heat, stirring constantly, until tapioca is translucent, about 10 minutes. Pour over fruit. Return to oven and bake 20 minutes more. Let cool, then chill thoroughly before serving.

❖ *TWO-TONE CRUMB PARFAIT* ❖

4 SERVINGS

⅔ cup natural liquid sweetener
3 tablespoons vegetable or soy margarine
2¾ cups soy milk
3 tablespoons arrowroot
1½ teaspoons vanilla extract *or* seeds from 3-inch piece
  vanilla bean

2 tablespoons unsweetened carob powder, lightly toasted
  (see note, p. 64)
5 tablespoons dry cake or cookie crumbs

Combine sweetener and margarine in medium-size saucepan and place over low heat until margarine is melted. Mix small amount of soy milk into arrowroot to make smooth paste. Whisk into sweetener mixture and cook over low heat until mixture begins to thicken. Immediately whisk in remaining soy milk and continue cooking, stirring constantly, until thickened. Remove from heat and stir in vanilla.

Transfer half of pudding mixture to mixing bowl. Whisk in carob powder. Divide carob mixture among four parfait glasses. Sprinkle with crumbs, reserving small amount of garnish. Top with vanilla pudding mixture and sprinkle with reserved crumbs. Chill until serving time.

Fresh Fruit Desserts

EASY BAKED APPLES

BAKED FRESH FRUIT

BAKED BANANAS JAMAICA

BERRY SURPRISE

BAKED FRUIT TAHITI

SPICED FRUIT DELIGHT

HAWAIIAN DELIGHT

POACHED PEARS IN FRESH ORANGE SAUCE

QUICK STUFFED STRAWBERRIES WITH FRESH BERRY SAUCE

Light and refreshing, fresh fruit desserts are often the best of all. They can end a meal or liven up a buffet brunch. Take advantage of seasonal bounty to use fresh berries and melons in the summer, pears and apples in the fall. Here are some delightful recipes to please the palate all year long.

❖ *EASY BAKED APPLES* ❖

A very simple but satisfying sweet that can be served as a light dessert or to accompany a lunch or dinner entree.

2 SERVINGS

2 baking apples
3 tablespoons natural liquid sweetener
Juice of ½ lemon
1 teaspoon ground cinnamon
¼ teaspoon ground allspice

Preheat oven to 375°F. Core apples. Peel top one third of each. Place apples in small, shallow baking dish. Combine sweetener, lemon juice, and spices and pour into hollowed apple cores. Add enough water to pan to just cover bottom. Bake until apples are tender when pierced with fork, basting several times during baking. Serve warm.

❖ *BAKED FRESH FRUIT* ❖

A lovely, light dessert, especially appropriate with brunch.

6 TO 8 SERVINGS

1 cup cake or cookie crumbs, lightly toasted
2 pears, cored and cut into ¼-inch-thick slices
2 peaches or nectarines, pitted, peeled, and cut into ¼-inch-thick slices
3 to 4 small apricots, peeled, pitted, and halved
½ cup Bing cherries, pitted
½ cup seedless green grapes
2 to 3 tablespoons natural liquid sweetener (optional)
1 teaspoon fresh lemon juice
1 teaspoon ground cinnamon
¼ teaspoon ground allspice
1 cup (more or less) unsweetened white grape juice or Amasake drink (page 166)

Preheat oven to 375°F. Grease 2-quart soufflé or baking dish and sprinkle bottom with half of crumbs. Arrange fruits over crumbs. Mix sweetener, lemon juice, and spices and drizzle over fruit. Top with remaining crumbs. Pour in grape juice or amasake to depth of ¼ inch. Cover fruit with waxed paper, then cover dish tightly with aluminum foil. Bake until fruit is tender, 30 to 40 minutes.

Remove waxed paper and foil. Place dish under broiler briefly to brown crumbs; watch carefully to prevent burning. Serve fruit warm or at room temperature.

❖ *BAKED BANANAS JAMAICA* ❖

Great as a last-minute dessert, or serve alongside a lunch or dinner entree.

4 SERVINGS

---

4 ripe bananas, peeled and halved lengthwise
1 tablespoon corn oil
1 to 2 tablespoons natural liquid sweetener or date sugar
Juice of 1 lemon or lime

Preheat oven to 400°F. Lightly grease (or spray with lecithin) baking dish large enough to hold bananas. Rub bananas with corn oil on all sides. Arrange decoratively in prepared baking dish. Drizzle with sweetener. Sprinkle with lemon or lime juice. Bake until bananas are softened and lightly browned. Serve warm.

VARIATION:

For a spiced version, mix ½ teaspoon ground cinnamon and ¼ teaspoon ground allspice into sweetener before drizzling over bananas.

❖ BERRY SURPRISE ❖

6 SERVINGS

1 cup fresh raspberries, blueberries, or blackberries
¼ cup fresh or reconstituted frozen unsweetened orange
    juice
½ cup whole wheat pastry flour or sweet brown rice flour
½ cup rolled oats
⅓ cup natural liquid sweetener
¼ cup corn oil
½ cup ground blanched almonds

Preheat oven to 400°F. Divide berries among six individual custard cups. Add 2 teaspoons orange juice to each cup. Combine flour, oats, sweetener, and oil to form crumbs. Blend in almonds. Top fruit with crumb mixture, dividing evenly. Bake until golden brown, about 20 minutes. Serve warm or at room temperature.

❖ BAKED FRUIT TAHITI ❖

This tropical fruit delight was inspired by a friend's lovingly detailed description of a dessert she first tasted during her Tahitian honeymoon.

8 SERVINGS

1 ripe mango, peeled and cut into medium-size chunks
9 ounces finely chopped fresh or canned unsweetened
    crushed pineapple
1 ripe papaya, peeled, seeded, and cut into chunks
3 tablespoons arrowroot
5 tablespoons unsweetened pineapple or other fruit juice
½ cup natural liquid sweetener
1 teaspoon vanilla extract *or* seeds from 1-inch piece
    vanilla bean
1 teaspoon ground cinnamon
2 medium-size or 3 small bananas, sliced and sprinkled
    with fresh lemon or lime juice
    Vanilla-flavored soy milk or fresh coconut milk

Preheat oven to 375°F. Lightly grease 9-inch square baking dish. Place mango, pineapple, and papaya in food processor fitted with a steel blade and blend until coarsely pureed. Mix arrowroot with enough fruit juice to make a paste; stir paste back into remaining fruit juice. Stir fruit juice mixture into pureed fruits along with sweetener, vanilla, and cinnamon. Stir in sliced bananas.

Spoon mixture into prepared pan and bake until top is bubbly and slightly browned, about 50 to 60 minutes. Place pan under broiler for 2 to 3 minutes if additional browning is desired. Let cool, then cover with plastic wrap. Refrigerate until serving time.

To serve, cut into squares. Place each square in shallow glass ice cream or pudding dish. Pour fresh vanilla-flavored soy milk or coconut milk around sides of fruit square.

VARIATION:

Prepare crumble topping from Berry Surprise (page 198). Spread in lightly greased pan and bake at 375°F until lightly browned, about 12 to 15 minutes. Spoon fruit mixture onto baked crumble and bake as directed.

❖ *SPICED FRUIT DELIGHT* ❖

8 SERVINGS

2 apples, peeled, cored, and cut into ¼-inch-thick slices
2 pears, cored and cut into ¼-inch-thick slices
4 ounces Bing cherries, pitted
2 tablespoons fresh lemon juice
3 cups unsweetened unfiltered apple juice
2 3-inch sticks cinnamon
2 cups fresh strawberries, raspberries, or blueberries

Combine apples, pears, and cherries in large bowl and sprinkle with lemon juice. Toss to coat evenly. Combine apple juice and cinnamon in medium-size saucepan and bring to boil. Boil until reduced by half, about 10 minutes. Let cool; remove cinnamon sticks. Add to fruit and stir to coat. Chill thoroughly. Stir in berries just before serving.

❖ HAWAIIAN DELIGHT ❖

Perfect for a large buffet. If you wish, you can serve the fruit in a hollowed-out watermelon shell.

15 TO 18 SERVINGS

6 cups seeded watermelon balls or cubes
4 cups honeydew melon balls or cubes
4 cups assorted fresh berries
1 fresh ripe pineapple, peeled, cored, and cut into cubes
8 ounces seedless green grapes
2 large seedless oranges or tangerines, peeled and sectioned
2 bananas, peeled, sliced, and sprinkled with fresh lemon juice
1 cup freshly grated or packaged unsweetened coconut, toasted
1 teaspoon natural alcohol-free rum flavoring

Combine all ingredients. Chill at least 1 hour before serving.

❖ POACHED PEARS IN FRESH ❖ ORANGE SAUCE

An elegant dessert, just right after a special dinner.

8 SERVINGS

8 ripe pears
1¼ cups fresh or reconstituted frozen unsweetened orange juice
½ teaspoon grated lemon peel
½ teaspoon ground cinnamon
¼ cup cold water
1½ teaspoons arrowroot
Quick Fresh Orange Sauce (see recipe)
Thin orange peel julienne and/or mint sprigs (garnish)

Preheat oven to 425°F. Peel pears; core from bottom, leaving stems intact. Arrange in small flameproof pan. Combine orange juice, lemon peel, and cinnamon and pour over pears. Place in oven until juices begin to boil. Reduce heat to 375°F and spoon juices over pears. Cover and bake until pears are tender, 15 to 20 minutes.

Carefully remove pears from pan. Place pan with juices over low heat. Combine water and arrowroot to form paste and whisk into juices. Increase heat to medium and cook, whisking constantly, until thickened and smooth.

Pour thickened juices into serving dish; arrange pears on top. Pour warm orange sauce over pears and swirl decoratively through juices. Garnish with orange peel and/or mint. Serve warm or at room temperature.

QUICK FRESH ORANGE SAUCE

MAKES ABOUT 1 CUP

⅔ cup natural liquid sweetener
½ cup fresh or reconstituted frozen unsweetened orange juice
2 teaspoons finely grated orange peel
½ teaspoon natural alcohol-free rum or brandy flavoring (optional)

Combine all ingredients except rum flavoring in small saucepan and bring to boil. Reduce heat and simmer until reduced and thickened. Remove from heat and stir in flavoring. Serve warm or at room temperature.

❖ QUICK STUFFED STRAWBERRIES ❖ WITH FRESH BERRY SAUCE

This light dessert is not only easy to prepare but low in calories and beautiful to serve.

MAKES 2½ DOZEN

---

30 medium-size to large strawberries

2 cups vanilla or preferred flavor Creamy Soy Whip (page 173)
1 pint raspberries

Fresh mint sprigs (garnish)

Rinse strawberries (do not soak) in cold water and pat dry. Hull and arrange on paper towels to drain. Starting from the point of each strawberry make a cut three quarters of the way to the bottom. Make second cut at 90° angle to first cut, dividing the strawberry into quarters. Refrigerate while preparing soy whip.

Fit pastry bag with small round pastry tip. Fill each strawberry with a swirl of soy whip.

Puree raspberries in blender of food processor. Strain to remove seeds if desired. Spread puree in decorative serving dish or on individual plates and arrange stuffed strawberries on top. Decorate sides of dish with 2 or 3 fresh mint sprigs.

Frozen Desserts

FROZEN AMBROSIA CUPS

SUMMER FRUIT SHERBET

APRICOT FREEZE

LUSCIOUS FROZEN AVOCADO CREME

REAL VANILLA BEAN ICE CREME

TANGY LEMON SHERBET

COCAMOCHA SHERBET

MANGO—PAPAYA SHERBET

BANANA—NUT SORBET

FROZEN PEACH SORBET WITH RASPBERRY SAUCE

CITRUS ICE

CRANBERRY—APPLE ICE

MOCHA ICE WITH VANILLA SOY WHIP

FROZEN ORANGE—BANANA POPS

W henever I serve a frozen concoction, there always seems to be a general consensus of amazement that it is actually homemade. Interestingly, while some cooks will tackle even the most intricate of recipes, they leave ice cream to commercial manufacturers.

If you are an avid ice cream lover, your tastebuds will tingle at the first bite of these easy-to-prepare frozen delights. Unlike their traditional counterparts, which rely on eggs and milk products for their velvety texture, these recipes are dairy-free. Soy milk and a small amount of oil or lecithin are combined to create a smooth, rich-tasting ice creme that is low in calories and contains no saturated fat or cholesterol. These mixtures also do not contain much sweetener, especially the sorbets made with fresh fruits.

NOTE: *In order to differentiate the recipes in this book from commercially prepared ice "creams," which must, by law, contain butterfat, I have used the term "creme" throughout. I have made a similar kind of distinction between sherbets and sorbets. The sherbets in this book contain soy milk or soy powder and thus are slightly more rich and creamy than the sorbets, which are lighter and made with fresh fruits and fruit juices.*

TIPS FOR SUCCESS

- All liquids used should be chilled before mixing.
- It's important that the mixture be well blended, especially when using liquid lecithin or oil.
- Ice cremes should be stirred or beaten in the blender or processor at least twice during the freezing process if an ice tray is being used. This keeps ice crystals from forming and results in a smooth consistency. Ice cremes can be stored in a covered container in the freezer for up to 10 days (though they're rarely around that long).
- Sherbets and sorbets should be stirred or beaten once before final freezing. If they are too hard to scoop into serving dishes, let stand at room temperature for 5 to 10 minutes before serv-

ing. (It is best to let sherbet stand for a short period anyway, because the slight warming heightens flavor.)

- These recipes use a different ratio of sweetener to liquid than most other frozen desserts. The sweetener is in syrup form to begin with and does not have to be cooked first, as granulated sugar often does. Traditional ice cream relies on egg yolks and cream for a smooth consistency. These desserts substitute liquid lecithin, corn oil, or agar-agar flakes and are thus dairy-free of saturated fat and cholesterol. They are also lower in calories, especially if made with liquid lecithin or agar-agar.

- In Europe, especially in Italy where delicious fresh fruit *granita* is served, very little if any sweetener is used in frozen ices. This results in a more crystallized consistency. (Additional beating with a spoon or in a food processor immediately before serving will help remedy this if you prefer a smoother texture.) When using any of the fresh-fruit ice or sorbet recipes below, omit the sweetener if desired and substitute an equal amount of unsweetened fruit juice.

- Experiment with your own favorite combinations of ingredients. Add crushed cookie or cake crumbs, unsweetened coconut, blanched and lightly toasted pistachios, almonds, macadamias, or pecans—up to 1 cup per quart. Although it's best to add these ingredients when the ice cremes are at least semifrozen, I have frozen them all at once with the liquid mixture when using an ice cream maker. They should be stirred into the ice tray after final beating.

- Remember that ice cremes must contain either liquid lecithin, oil, or agar-agar for a smooth consistency, but that too much will keep the ice creme from freezing completely. One quart should never contain more than 2 tablespoons lecithin or ¼ cup corn oil.

- Frozen desserts can be made in electric or hand-cranked ice cream makers or in freezer trays. It is certainly not necessary to invest in an ice cream maker, though it does eliminate the need to restir the mixture during the freezing process to ensure smooth texture. When using an electric or hand-cranked ice cream maker, prepare the mixture according to the recipe and then follow the manufacturer's directions. To freeze in an ice cube tray, prepare the mixture and pour into trays without the partitions. Let freeze until just the edges have frozen. Remove from freezer and beat until smoooth with a wooden spoon, food processor, or mixer. Spoon the mixture back into trays and refreeze. Repeat this procedure a few times during freezing for soy ice cremes and once for sorbets or sherbets (beat a final time immediately before serving). Sorbets and sherbets should be served within a day or two of preparation, whereas soy ice creme can be stored up to 10 days. If crystals begin to form in storage simply let the ice creme soften slightly at room temperature, beat until smooth, and refreeze.

❖ *FROZEN AMBROSIA CUPS* ❖

4 SERVINGS

---

4 large seedless oranges

½ cup strawberries or raspberries, sliced

⅓ cup shredded unsweetened coconut

1 pint Summer Fruit Sherbet (recipe follows) or Citrus Ice (page 215)

Mint sprigs

Cut top third of oranges off and retain tops. Scoop out insides and peel membranes away from orange sections. Place orange pulp in a food processor or blender. Set orange shells and tops aside.

Add sliced berries and coconut to orange pulp and whirl for 1 to 2 minutes or until ingredients are well mixed. Add sherbet or ice and blend until smooth. Spoon mixture into orange shells, cover with waxed paper, and freeze. If desired, top shells with orange tops, then freeze.

To serve, let stand at room temperature for 5 minutes. Garnish with fresh mint.

❖ *SUMMER FRUIT SHERBET* ❖

10-12 SERVINGS

---

2 cups cold soy milk

2 cups cold water

1½ cups mixed fresh citrus juices (lime, lemon, orange and/ or grapefruit)

2 bananas, peeled

4 ounces fresh or unsweetened frozen berries

½ cup chopped ripe melon

2 tablespoons liquid lecithin

Combine all ingredients in food processor or blender and whirl until smooth. Transfer mixture to ice trays or an ice cream maker and freeze according to directions on page 207.

•:• *APRICOT FREEZE* •:•

Spoon into decorative muffin cups and freeze for individual servings. Topped with soy whip, these frozen cups are perfect for a buffet dessert.

18 SERVINGS

17 ounces apricots, pitted, peeled, and chopped
 9 ounces fresh pineapple, finely chopped
 3 medium-size bananas, peeled
 1 cup fresh or reconstituted frozen unsweetened orange
   juice
¼ cup natural liquid sweetener (optional)
 1 teaspoon fresh lemon juice
   Creamy Soy Whip (page 173) or Tofu Whip (page 175)
   (garnish)

Combine all ingredients in blender (in batches if necessary) or food processor and whirl until well blended but not completely smooth. Spoon mixture into muffin cups, three quarters full. Freeze until hardened.

To serve, let cups stand at room temperature for 5 minutes. Top with a decorative swirl of soy or tofu whip.

•:• *LUSCIOUS FROZEN AVOCADO CREME* •:•

A delicious, rich-tasting ice creme.

4 SERVINGS

 2 large ripe avocados, peeled and pitted
½ cup cold soy milk
½ cup natural liquid sweetener
 1 tablespoon liquid lecithin
 1 teaspoon fresh lemon or lime juice

   Sliced kiwi (garnish)

Combine all ingredients in blender or food processor and whirl until smooth and creamy. Pour mixture into ice trays or an ice cream maker and freeze according to directions on page 207.

To serve, scoop ice creme into dishes and garnish with sliced kiwi.

❖ *REAL VANILLA BEAN ICE CREME* ❖

Real vanilla bean seeds are an important ingredient in this delicious, smooth-textured ice creme. Serve garnished with fresh fruit or a sauce (topping with nuts if desired), or try one of the variations.

6 SERVINGS

---

1 4-inch piece vanilla bean or 2 teaspoons vanilla extract
1 cup soy milk powder, mixed with 2½ cup water, or 4 cups soy milk
¾ cup natural liquid sweetener
¼ cup corn oil
⅛ teaspoon salt

Slit vanilla bean open and squeeze seeds out into soy milk (or add extract).

Combine all ingredients in blender or food processor and whirl until well blended.

Pour mixture into ice trays or ice cream maker and freeze according to directions on page 207.

To serve, scoop into dishes and garnish with sliced fresh fruit or berries. For special occasions, drizzle ice creme with Carob Glaze (page 128) or another sauce.

VARIATIONS:

Carob Fudge Swirl: Prepare vanilla ice creme mixture and freeze. Make Carob Glaze (page 128) and swirl into semifrozen vanilla ice creme with a knife after the final mixing stage (if using a freezer tray). If using an ice cream maker, let ice creme soften slightly if necessary before transferring to freezer container. Pour cooled carob glaze over ice creme and swirl through. Spoon into container and store in freezer.

Maple–Nut: Use pure maple syrup as the liquid sweetener when making the vanilla ice creme. If using an ice cream maker, add 7 ounces chopped nuts (pecans, walnuts, or macadamias) to the mixture before starting the motor or cranking. If using an ice tray, add the chopped nuts after the final beating during the freezing process.

Carob–Mint: Use only a 1-inch piece of vanilla bean or 1 teaspoon extract. Stir ⅔ cup lightly toasted unsweetened carob powder into oil, then add to other ingredients in the processor or blender. Add 1 teaspoon natural mint flavoring and follow recipe for vanilla ice creme.

Mocha–Carob Chip: Decrease vanilla bean or extract as for Carob–Mint ice creme, above. Add 2 tablespoons powdered grain coffee substitute to oil before adding to other ingredients. If using an ice cream maker, add unsweetened carob chips to ice cream maker container along with mocha mixture and freeze according to manufacturer's directions. To freeze in an ice tray, stir in chips during final beating or, if a smaller chip is preferred, add chips to processor or blender for a second or two.

Peanutty Crunch: Reduce vanilla as for Carob–Mint ice creme, above. Omit corn oil; add 1 tablespoon liquid lecithin. Add ¾ cup natural unsalted crunchy-style peanut butter to ice creme mixture before freezing in tray or ice cream maker. For special occasions, add ½ cup unsweetened carob chips as in Mocha–Chip variation, above.

Fresh Strawberry: Reduce vanilla as for Carob–Mint ice creme, above. Add 1 pint sliced strawberries to ice creme mixture and follow directions for tray or ice cream maker freezing method.

Fresh Raspberry: Same as Fresh Strawberry, above, using 2 cups fresh raspberries to ice creme mixture. Add 1 teaspoon finely grated lemon peel if desired.

Cookies-and-Creme: This is a great way to use leftover cookie crumbs. Use a variety; gingersnap or carob chip crumbs are especially delicious. Add 1 cup crushed cookie crumbs to ice creme mixture and freeze.

❖ *TANGY LEMON SHERBET* ❖

A refreshing, light dessert. For special occasions serve in gingersnap cups (see serving suggestion below).

6 SERVINGS

2 cups soy milk
½ cup natural liquid sweetener
Juice of 2 large lemons
½ teaspoon liquid lecithin
2 teaspoons finely grated lemon peel

Fresh mint sprigs (garnish)

Combine soy milk, sweetener, lemon juice, and lecithin in blender and whirl until smooth. Stir in grated lemon peel. Freeze in ice tray or ice cream maker according to directions on page 207.

To serve, make Gingersnaps (page 48). While still warm, mold cookies over bottoms of muffin cups to form a cup shape. Serve a scoop of sherbet in each, garnishing with a mint sprig.

❖ *COCAMOCHA SHERBET* ❖

10 SERVINGS

½ cup unsweetened cocoa powder
¾ cup natural liquid sweetener
⅛ teaspoon salt
2 teaspoons liquid lecithin
1 teaspoon vanilla extract
1 tablespoon powdered grain coffee substitute
3½ cup soy milk

Combine all ingredients except soy milk in blender or food processor and whirl until well mixed. Add soy milk and blend well. Freeze in ice tray or ice cream maker according to directions on page 207.

VARIATIONS:
Add ½ cup crushed cookie crumbs or unsweetened carob chips to ice cream maker along with sherbet mixture, or add crumbs or chips to semifrozen sherbet during final beating if freezing in ice tray.

❖ *MANGO–PAPAYA SHERBET* ❖

An exotic, refreshing frozen dessert that I especially enjoy serving after a spicy meal.

MAKES 1½ PINTS

2 ripe mangoes, peeled, pitted, and sliced
2 ripe papayas, peeled, seeded, and sliced
6 tablespoons natural liquid sweetener
6 tablespoons cold water
2 tablespoons fresh lemon juice
1 teaspoon finely grated lemon peel
½ cup cold soy milk

Combine all ingredients except soy milk in blender or food processor and whirl until smooth and well mixed. Add soy milk and blend well. Pour into ice cream maker or ice tray and freeze according to directions on page 207.

❖ *BANANA–NUT SORBET* ❖

MAKES 1¾ PINTS

3 medium-size bananas, peeled
1 cup cold water
¾ cup fresh or reconstituted frozen unsweetened orange, pineapple, or apple juice
3 tablespoons natural liquid sweetener
1 teaspoon fresh lemon juice
5 ounces pecans, chopped

Combine all ingredients except nuts in blender or food processor and mix until smooth. Stir in chopped nuts. Pour mixture into an ice cream maker and freeze according to manufacturer's directions. To freeze in an ice tray, pour mixture into tray and freeze until semisolid. Beat in a food processor or blender, or with a wooden spoon, and stir in nuts. Freeze until hardened.

Let stand at room temperature at least 5 minutes or until slightly softened before serving.

VARIATIONS:

Add 1 to 2 teaspoons natural rum flavoring.

Banana–Peanut Butter Sorbet: Don't make a face—it's delicious! Use 1 cup unsweetened apple juice or cider. Omit lemon juice. Add 1 teaspoon vanilla extract. Blend in ¼ cup unsalted natural crunchy-style peanut butter. Omit chopped nuts.

❖ *FROZEN PEACH SORBET WITH* ❖ *RASPBERRY SAUCE*

A light dessert after a summer meal—this frozen delight resembles the classic Peach Melba.

MAKES ABOUT 1½ PINTS

---

4 ripe peaches, peeled, pitted, and sliced
9 tablespoons cold water
6 tablespoons natural liquid sweetener
1 tablespoon fresh lemon juice
½ teaspoon ground cinnamon (optional)
1 pint fresh or unsweetened frozen raspberries
1 to 2 tablespoons natural liquid sweetener (optional)

Creamy Soy Whip (page 173) and fresh raspberries (garnish)

Combine peaches, water, 6 tablespoons sweetener, lemon juice, and cinnamon in blender or food processor and whirl until well mixed and smooth. Pour into ice cream maker or ice tray and freeze according to directions on page 207.

Meanwhile, puree raspberries, adding sweetener if desired.

To serve, scoop sorbet into dishes and pour raspberry sauce around sides. Top each scoop with a small rosette of soy whip and a few fresh raspberries.

❖ CITRUS ICE ❖

MAKES 2 QUARTS

2 cups water
¾ to 1 cup natural liquid sweetener
grated peel of ½ grapefruit

4 cups mixed fresh or reconstituted frozen
unsweetened citrus juices (grapefruit, orange, lemon,
and/or lime)
⅓ cup fresh lemon juice

Mint sprigs, sliced kiwi, or strawberries (garnish)

Combine water and sweetener in saucepan, bring to boil, and let boil for 5 minutes. Remove from heat. Stir in grated peel. Let cool.

Combine cooled syrup, mixed citrus juices, and lemon juice. Pour into ice trays or an ice cream maker and freeze according to directions on page 207.

To serve, let ice stand at room temperature for 5 minutes before serving. Scoop into parfait or wine glasses. Garnish with fresh mint sprigs, kiwi, or strawberries.

❖ *CRANBERRY–APPLE ICE* ❖

MAKES ABOUT 2 QUART

2 pounds fresh cranberries, rinsed and drained
4 cup unfiltered apple juice or cider
⅔ cup natural liquid sweetener
1 teaspoon grated orange peel

Combine cranberries, 2 cups apple juice, and sweetener in medium-size saucepan. Cook until cranberries are softened, about 7 to 10 minutes. Remove from heat and put cranberry mixture through food mill or puree in food processor. Add remaining apple juice and orange peel and chill thoroughly. Pour into ice trays and freeze according to directions on page 207.

❖ *MOCHA ICE WITH VANILLA SOY WHIP* ❖

I first tasted the original version (an incredible collaboration of espresso and unsweetened whipped cream) quite a few years ago in Rome. As a starving artist I always managed to find the means for a daily dose of coffee ice and cream. This recipe substitutes a good-quality decaf or grain coffee substitute and soy whip with excellent results. Unlike sorbets, ice cream, and sherbets, in this frozen dessert ice crystals are desirable and should resemble long chips.

MAKES 1½ PINTS

½ cup natural liquid sweetener
1 tablespoon unsweetened carob powder, lightly toasted (see note, p. 64)
2 cups cold strong decaffeinated coffee (see note, p. 217) or grain coffee substitute
1 cup cold water
1 teaspoon vanilla extract or seeds from 1-inch piece vanilla bean
Vanilla-flavored Creamy Soy Whip (page 173) (garnish)

Combine sweetener and carob powder in food processor or blender and mix well. Add coffee, water, and vanilla and whirl until well mixed. Pour into an ice tray or other metal container. Freeze 1 hour. Stir gently with wooden spoon, being careful not to break ice crystals too finely.

Freeze an additional hour and serve; if ice is too hard, let soften at room temperature for 5 to 10 minutes. Spoon into glass dishes and top with a rosette of soy whip flavored with vanilla.

NOTE: *Purchase good-quality French roast or Mocha Java decaf—made with the European "spring-water extraction process"—available at most coffee and tea stores.*

❖ *FROZEN ORANGE–BANANA POPS* ❖

Not just for kids!

6 SERVINGS

3 medium-size bananas, peeled and mashed (about 2 cups)
1 cup fresh or reconstituted frozen unsweetened orange juice
¼ cup water
2 tablespoons natural liquid sweetener (optional)
1 teaspoon fresh lemon or lime juice

Blend all ingredients with wire whisk or in food processor. Divide mixture among six 5-ounce paper cups. When almost frozen, place wooden ice pop stick or small plastic spoon in center of each and let freeze completely.

To serve pops, let stand at room temperature for a few minutes and tear off paper cups.

VARIATIONS:

Fill cups with any of the preceding sorbet or sherbet mixtures.

Confections

CAROB–NUT CHEWS
CRUNCHY PEANUT BUTTER FUDGE
FRUITY COCONUT DROPS
MOCHI MUNCHIES
SESAME MORSELS

Bite-size nibbles to serve as a meal's sweet finale or to satisfy an impulsive sweet tooth. These recipes use only nutritious ingredients, but remember—calories are calories, and these are still rich sweets!

❖ *CAROB–NUT CHEWS* ❖

MAKES 5 DOZEN 1-INCH SQUARES

---

1 cup unsweetened, unsalted peanut butter
¾ cup natural liquid sweetener
1 cup unsweetened carob powder, lightly toasted (see
   note, p. 64)
1 cup sesame seeds, lightly toasted
1 cup hulled unsalted sunflower seeds
½ cup freshly ground or unsweetened packaged coconut
½ cup chopped unsulfured dried fruit

Lightly grease 8-inch square pan or spray with lecithin. Heat peanut butter and sweetener together in medium-size saucepan over medium heat. Stir in carob powder until mixture is smooth. Remove from heat and stir in remaining ingredients. Spread mixture in prepared pan and refrigerate at least 2 hours. Cut into 1-inch squares. Cover with plastic wrap and store in refrigerator.

❖ *CRUNCHY PEANUT BUTTER FUDGE* ❖

This protein-filled fudge is quick and easy to prepare. It's so rich tasting that it's hard to believe it's so good for you!

MAKES 18 TO 20 SQUARES

---

2 cups crunchy-style unsweetened, unsalted peanut butter
5 ounces powder soy milk, lightly toasted, or Nutquik (see
   note)
¼ cup natural liquid sweetener
⅔ cup granola or unsweetened puffed rice, millet, or
   wheat

Lightly spray 8-inch square pan with liquid lecithin. Combine peanut butter, soy milk powder, and sweetener in food processor or mixing bowl and blend well. Stir in cereal. Spread mixture in prepared pan. Chill for at least 1 hour. Cut into squares and serve.

NOTE: *Nutquik is a brand of soy milk powder available in health food stores.*

❖ *FRUITY COCONUT DROPS* ❖

A food processor really comes in handy in the chopping and mixing of these delicious confections.

MAKES ABOUT 4 DOZEN

---

1 cup pitted prunes
1 cup pitted dates
1 cup dark raisins
1 cup golden raisins
½ cup freshly grated or unsweetened packaged coconut
¼ cup raw wheat germ
2 tablespoons fresh orange juice
1 teaspoon grated orange peel
9 ounces pecans, finely chopped

Combine prunes and dates in food processor fitted with steel blade. Chop finely. Add all remaining ingredients except 4 ounces of the nuts. Process only until mixture holds together, about 1 minute. Roll mixture into small balls or egg shapes and roll in reserved chopped nuts. Store airtight at room temperature.

❖ *MOCHI MUNCHIES* ❖

These treats were inspired by a moist sweet rice cake I first tasted at a Japanese tea party. Though mochi is usually made from pounded sweet rice, try experimenting with other grains such as millet or couscous.

Cooked sweet brown rice
Natural liquid sweetener (optional)
Finely chopped nuts or unsweetened carob powder
Ground cinnamon (optional)

Place cooked rice in wooden bowl or on large wooden cutting board. Use wooden mallet or pestle (see note) to pound rice into a sticky mass,

(recipe continues)

dipping mallet into cold water occasionally if it becomes too sticky. If desired, add natural liquid sweetener to taste. Form mixture into small balls. Roll in chopped nuts or carob powder, flavored with cinnamon if desired.

VARIATIONS:

Form rice into cylinder. Wrap in plastic or waxed paper and refrigerate. When chilled, cut into ½-inch-thick slices and sauté until golden in small amount of margarine or corn oil. Slices can also be arranged on greased or lecithin-sprayed baking sheet and baked at 350°F until golden. Serve slices plain or lightly drizzled with natural liquid sweetener, glaze, or fresh fruit sauce.

NOTE: *Some health food stores carry a special mallet for pounding mochi.*

•:• SESAME MORSELS •:•

MAKES 18 TO 20

---

8 ounces pitted prunes
8 ounces pitted dates
⅓ cup raisins
½ cup sesame seeds, lightly toasted

Combine dried fruits in food processor fitted with steel blade and blend until mixture forms paste. Mold into small balls and roll in sesame seeds. Store airtight at room temperature.

Index

ABOUT THE AUTHOR

Cherie Baker is a professional cook, caterer, and cooking school teacher who has been pursuing a healthier diet for the last ten years. She honed her pastry-making skills as a consultant and chef at the Yarrowstalk, a natural foods restaurant in Boulder, Colorado, and she has been refining them ever since as a free-lance chef and teacher in Philadelphia and California. She currently lives in Los Angeles.